Stories for sharing

Charles Arcodia is a high school teacher with twelve years experience in the fields of Religious Education and Personal Development.

He lives in Brisbane with his wife and two children and is presently involved in post-graduate studies at the Australian Catholic University—Queensland.

His other publications include—a history text: *The Story of Humankind* (William Brooks, 1984); a simulation game: *If Fairness was the Name of the Game* (Aust. Catholic Relief, 1986); and a prayer book: *Count Me In* (Boolarong Publications, 1991).

Stories
for
Sharing

With Themes and Discussion Starters
for Teachers and Speakers

Charles
Arcodia

E. J. DWYER

For
KRISTY-MARIE

First published 1991 by
E. J. Dwyer (Australia) Pty Ltd
3/32-72 Alice Street
Newtown NSW 2042
Australia

National Library of Australia
Cataloguing-in-Publication data

Stories for sharing.

ISBN 0 85574 348 4.

1. Children's sermons. 2. Homiletical illustrations.
I. Arcodia, Charles. II. Title.

252.53

Illustrations by Bev Aisbett
Cover and text design by Katrina Rendell
Typeset in 11/12 pt Garamond by Solo Typesetting, South Australia
Printed in Australia by The Book Printer, Maryborough, Victoria

FOREWORD

A Jewish writer once said: 'God so loved stories, He made man and woman.' Stories tell us about who we are and link us together as a human family. When we hear the magic words 'Once upon a time . . .' we can settle back and enjoy a tale which makes us laugh, cry, reflect or all three!

When friends meet they tell stories. Stories enable us to imagine other possibilities for being a human person in our world. People remember stories long after they have forgotten the printed word. No wonder that Jesus used stories to describe the Kingdom of God—his dream for a new time of creation in the world. The parables of Jesus are stories which both invite and challenge us to explore opportunities for a new relationship with God as Abba and our brothers and sisters. 'The Kingdom of God is like . . .' says Jesus because all stories are really symbols for our imagination.

It is a pleasure to write this foreword for Charles Arcodia's collection of stories. I hope that these stories will enrich the lives of many people who read and hear them. Isaiah beautifully expresses the cycle of the word which flows from the mouth of God through the universe and returns to its Source. (Isaiah 55: 10–11.) May these stories, like the word of God, energize the listeners to be storytellers of life.

Kevin Treston

Getting the most out of this book

You may wish to read these stories simply for enjoyment or personal reflection. To help those who would like to use the stories in classes, homilies, group discussions, or speeches, they have been indexed by themes. However, depending on how they are approached, the stories may illustrate a number of points. The 'Reflection and Discussion' questions offer some directions for thought and group discussion, with links to Scripture.

CONTENTS

Chapters and themes

THEMES

ACKNOWLEDGEMENTS

The author gratefully acknowledges the use of material from the following works. Every effort has been made to locate the sources of quoted material and to obtain authority for its use.

'The Rabbi and the Soapmaker' adapted from a story in *Rabbinic Wisdom and Jewish Values* by W. Silverman. © 1971 Reprinted with permission of Union of American Hebrew Congregations, New York.

'The Fox and the Vineyard' from *Our Masters Taught: Rabbinic Stories and Sayings* by Jacob J. Petuchowski. © 1982 Reprinted by permission of The Crossroad Publishing Company, New York.

'The Cat in the Lifeboat', 'What Happened to Charles' copr. © 1956 James Thurber, 1984, Helen Thurber, from *Further Fables for Our Time*, pub. by Simon and Schuster; 'The Owl who was God' copr. © 1940 James Thurber, 1968, Helen Thurber, from *Fables for Our Time*, pub. by Harper & Row; 'The Last Flower' copr. © 1939 James Thurber, copr. © 1967, Helen Thurber and Rosemary A. Thurber, from *The Last Flower*, pub. by Harper & Row.
The above four stories by James Thurber also appear in *Vintage Thurber*, Vols. I and II, © 1963. Reprinted by permission of Hamish Hamilton, London.

'The Tower' and 'The Sound of the Song' from an unpublished manuscript by Graeme Smith. © 1988.

'The Chief Rabbi' from *The Gates of the Forest* by E. Wiesel © 1982 Schocken Books, New York.

'The Discarded Chair' from *Fairytales and the Kingdom of God* by A. Whitman © 1982 Dove Publications, New Mexico.

INTRODUCTION

Storytelling has always been central to Christianity. The gospels are full of stories Jesus told to communicate his understanding of certain truths about life and about God. But teaching with stories is not just for the Christian, as each religious tradition has its own stories to tell. In these pages you will find stories from a variety of sources. I have drawn from the Christian, Buddhist and Hindu traditions, but you will also find Chinese fables, Sufi tales, Hasidic yarns and modern-day parables.

Students often ask whether these stories are true. The answer very much depends on their understanding of truth as there are many kinds of truth. Did the events in these stories actually happen? No, probably not. So the stories may not be 'true', but there certainly is 'truth' in the stories. Religious truth can often be better illustrated in a fable or contemporary parable. In *A Small Town is a World*, David Kossoff explains why:

Here is a story about Parable, who was one of twins, his brother being Truth. When young they looked alike but as they grew they became less alike and went different ways. Parable was the better observer of men and women and more amenable to change. Truth, when young, went always naked and people did not mind. To see a little naked Truth did no one any great harm. But when Truth grew up and became man-size and still went naked his life was hard and people kept away from him. They were shocked and frightened by naked Truth and wouldn't have him in their homes and protected their children from him. And thus it was. One day Parable came along . . . From head to foot he was a joy to behold. Of many colors were his clothes and his hat was finest silk. His shoes were of the softest leather and he approached without noise. "What is this, brother?" he said, "so sad, so long-faced, naked and cold."

Truth told him, truthfully, of his sad life. "Everybody avoids me," he said. "I have no place anywhere. I am old and finished."

"Rubbish!" replied Parable. "We are the same age. And I am welcome everywhere. People don't mind me one bit. You see, brother, people are funny. They don't like things naked and straightforward. They like things fancied up and a bit fake, like me. Come, we are still the same size, we are twins. I will give you some of my finery. I've got lots, and it will change your life."

And it did. Soon the twins were inseparable. You could hardly tell them apart. And Truth, dressed like Parable, was welcome everywhere.[1]

So if we dress truth up and put it in a parable, it becomes concrete and more acceptable. It is often difficult to grasp abstract ideas because most of us think in pictures. William Barclay makes such an observation. How do you explain 'beauty' or 'goodness'? You can use words to describe and define these concepts, but the concept may not become any clearer. Everyone can recognize, however, the goodness in a person or the beauty in a sunrise. The power of the story is that it presents us with a familiar truth in a simple, direct and vivid *picture* and thus invites us to participate and explore, regardless of age and experience of life.

Walter Pater, the nineteenth-century critic, said you cannot tell people the truth; you can only put them in a position in which they can discover it for themselves. The story allows us to make that discovery for ourselves. A young child may hear a wonderful tale of magic and adventure while a more mature person will hear the same tale and see in it a reflection of the human condition. Truth shared in this creative, gentle way, is difficult to ignore. It will challenge our values and our understandings of life, and push us beyond the ordinary to a world where contemplation and mystery take over.[2]

These stories should be told rather than read. *In The Way of the Storyteller*, Ruth Sawyer paints this valid picture:

There is a kind of death to every story when it leaves the speaker and becomes impaled for all time on . . . the printed page. To take it from this page, to create it again into living substance, this is the challenge for the storyteller.[3]

Once the story is told, try not to be concerned whether the hearer understands all of what it means. You cannot predict the impact of a story because those who hear it respond from their own experiences of life. Listeners will hear what they are ready to hear—no more! One further point—resist the urge to explain the subtleties in the story. Good stories, well told, need no explanation; often silence is all that is required.

This book offers stories of life, of hope, of wonder, of peace, of prayer, of understanding, of love. They will take you from the scientific and the abstract and introduce you to the spiritual and contemplative world where mystery, metaphor and symbol abound. I have enjoyed collecting these stories; I hope you enjoy reading and sharing them.

1. D. Kossoff, *A Small Town is a World*, Robson Banks Ltd., London, 1979.
2. S. Beauman (RSM) *Story and Religious Education* self published—no date.
3. R. Sawyer, *The Way of the Storyteller*, Penguin Books, London, 1976.

──── ▪ *The Collector* ▪ ────

Once upon a time, there was a very rich man who lived in a beautiful palace. He loved jewels, which he collected, constantly adding more pieces to his wonderful hoard. He kept all of them securely locked away, hidden from any eyes but his own.

Now the rich man had a friend who visited him one day and who expressed interest in seeing the gems.

"I would be delighted to take them out, so that I, too, could look at them," said the rich man.

So the collection was brought out, and the two of them feasted their eyes on the beautiful treasure for a long time, lost in admiration.

When the time came for him to leave, the rich man's guest said, "Thank you for giving me the treasure!"

"Do not thank me for something which you have not got," gasped the rich man, "for I have not given you the jewels! They are not yours at all."

His friend answered, "As you know, I have had as much pleasure from looking at the treasure as you, so there is no difference between us, as you, yourself, only look at them — except that you have the trouble and expense of finding, buying and looking after them."

▪ *Themes* ▪

Enjoyment–Happiness–Wealth

▪ *For reflection and discussion* ▪

1. What else can the rich man do with the jewels apart from looking at them?

2. Do you think the rich man's friend has a point when he says: 'Thank you for giving me the treasure'?

3. Do you think this story demonstrates well the uselessness of hoarding things? Why?

4. Read Matthew 6:24–31. What does Jesus promise to do for us in these passages?

A Life of Cheese
and Crackers

There was once a lady who scrimped and saved for years in order to take an ocean cruise. At long last, she had saved enough money to pay for her ticket. However, there was not much money left for luxuries. She nevertheless decided to go. "For I will take along a large supply of cheese and cracker biscuits," she thought, "and eat them in my cabin. That way it won't cost as much."

This is just what she did. She went on the cruise and had a fine time. At mealtimes, when the other passengers went to the dining room, she went to her cabin and ate cheese and crackers. She consoled herself with the knowledge that she had saved just enough money for one fine dinner. On her last night aboard she was going to splurge and have a gourmet meal!

The last night finally arrived, and she dressed in her best clothes. Finally, she was to eat with the other passengers in the dining room. With great anticipation, she ordered the most delicious meal. "Oh," she said, "the sacrifice was worthwhile."

At the end of the meal, she called the waiter and asked for her bill. The waiter looked at her in great surprise. "Madam," he said, "didn't you know that all of your meals were included in the price of your ticket?"

▪ Themes ▪

Enjoyment – Lost opportunity – Life experience

▪ *For reflection and discussion* ▪

1. What feelings do you think the woman experienced when she realized her mistake?

2. John Lennon (of the Beatles) once said: 'Life is what happens to you when you are busy making other plans.' Do you think this is true?

3. Why do you think the story is called *A LIFE of Cheese and Crackers*—not just *A TRIP on Cheese and Crackers*?

The Fox and
the Vineyard

A fox had discovered a vineyard—but the vineyard was surrounded by a fence on all sides. The fox did indeed find a hole in the fence through which he wanted to enter. Yet the hole was too narrow, and he did not succeed. So the fox fasted for three days until he became quite slim, and thus he managed to get through the hole.

Then he ate the grapes. But, in doing so, he again became fat. When the fox was ready to leave the vineyard again, he did not succeed in getting through the hole. So he fasted for another three days to become slim; and when he had done so, he managed to get out of the vineyard.

Once outside, he turned toward the vineyard and said, "Vineyard, vineyard, how good you are, and how good are your fruits! All that is within you is beautiful and praiseworthy! But of what use are you? The way one enters you is also the way in which one leaves you."

And so it is with the world.

▪ Themes ▪

Short-term benefits—Material gains

▪ For reflection and discussion ▪

1. 'The way one enters you is also the way in which one leaves you—and so it is with the world.' What do you understand by this statement?

2. Why do people often make the acquiring of things their top priority?

3. Read I Timothy 6:6–10, 17–19. Why is it that love of money can be the source of all evil?

The Rabbi and the Soapmaker

A Rabbi and a Soapmaker went for a walk together. The Soapmaker asked, "What good is religion? Look at all the trouble and misery of the world after thousands of years of teaching about goodness, truth, and peace—after all the prayers and sermons. If religion is so good for people, why should this be?"

The Rabbi said nothing. They continued walking until he noticed a child playing in the gutter. Then the Rabbi said, "Look at that child; you say that soap makes people clean, but see the dirt on that youngster. Of what good is soap? With all the soap in the world, the child is still filthy. I wonder how effective soap is after all?"

The Soapmaker protested and said, "But, Rabbi, soap can't do any good unless it is used."

"Exactly," replied the Rabbi. "So it is with religion."

▪ Themes ▪

Religion—Living by faith—Results

▪ For reflection and discussion ▪

1. Answer the Soapmaker's question: 'What good is religion'?

2. In what way does religion need to be 'used'?

3. Read Isaiah 43:1−7. What does God promise to those who are faithful to Him?

A Lesson for the King's Minder

A King was once walking in his garden when he stumbled over a blind man sleeping beside a bush. As the blind man awoke, he said: "You clumsy oaf! Have you no eyes, that you must trample upon the sons of men?"

One of the King's minders shouted in reply, "Your blindness is equalled only by your stupidity! Since you cannot see, you should be doubly careful of whom you are accusing of heedlessness."

"If by that you mean," said the blind man, "that I should not criticize a King, it is you who should realize your shallowness."

"And why should a King listen to the preaching of a blind man?" continued the minder.

"Precisely because it is the shielding of people of any category from criticism appropriate to them which is responsible for their downfall. It is the burnished metal which shines most brightly, the knife struck with the whetstone which cuts best, and the exercised arm which can lift the weight."

▪ Themes ▪

Constructive criticism – Self-evaluation

▪ For reflection and discussion ▪

1. What does the blind man mean when he says: 'It is the burnished metal which shines most brightly?'

2. Can any form of criticism ever be constructive?

3. Is it true that we learn by listening to the perception others have of us? Has this been your experience?

— ▪ *Come to the Edge* ▪ —

On top of a mountain there lived a family of eagles. It was a very high mountain which overlooked the surrounding country-side. From their vantage point they could see the village below, with its winding stream and farmland in the distance.

One day the mother-eagle looked at her young in the nest and said, "The time has come. You must learn to fly!"

"But how?" replied the young ones with more than a little uneasiness in their voices.

"You must go to the edge of the cliff," said the mother, "and throw yourself forward into the wind."

The young eagles looked at each other with anxious eyes. They walked to the edge, looked down very carefully and quickly scrambled back to the safety of the nest.

The next day mother-eagle told her young once again that the time had come for them to fly.

"It's far too high," said one of the young eagles.

"We might fall," said another.

"I'm frightened," said a third.

But mother-eagle was insistent. "Come to the edge," she urged repeatedly. "Come to the edge, don't be frightened."

When they gradually came, she gently pushed them.

And as they spread their wings, the wind lifted them and they flew.

▪ *Themes* ▪

Trust – Fear – Risk – Learning – Mother-love – Training

▪ *For reflection and discussion* ▪

1. What is one thing you fear?

2. What are some of the fears which prevent you from following Christ?

3. Why do many people find the 'leap of faith' a difficult one to make?

The Atheist

The word had gone around in the little Eastern European town that one of its most respected citizens, Abraham the cobbler, had become an out-and-out atheist. The whole town was shaken by the news; it was the sole topic of conversation all over. Nevertheless, all admitted that it was hearsay. No one had spoken directly to Abraham about it. It was still only rumor, even though a shocking one.

On the following Sabbath, however, it became clear to everyone in town that for the first time in thirty years Abraham the cobbler did not sit in his customary seat in the synagogue. Could he be sick? No, for when the services were over, they found that Abraham was walking quietly in the street, the very picture of health.

All stared, and finally Yussel the tailor, with a sudden burst of bravery, pushed forward and accused the cobbler. "Abraham," he cried, "there is a rumor that you have become an atheist. And you were not at the synagogue just now. Is this true? Are you indeed an atheist?" Abraham looked quietly at Yussel and turned away without a word.

Everyone looked after him in consternation, and by the next day it was clear that no work would be done in the town unless this matter was cleared up. So a delegation was appointed, with Yussel the tailor as its head, and it was understood that they were to face Abraham in his shop and insist on an answer once and for all.

In they went and Yussel said loudly, "Abraham, we must have an answer. You cannot leave matters as they are. Tell me, are you now an atheist?"

Abraham looked up from the shoe he was mending and said quietly, "Yes, I am!"

Astonished at the quick and unequivocal answer, Yussel said, "Then why didn't you say so when I asked you yesterday?"

Abraham's eyes grew wide with horror: "You wanted me to say I was an atheist on the Sabbath?"

▪ *Themes* ▪

Faith–Religion–Belief

▪ *For reflection and discussion* ▪

1. Do you think there are many people like Abraham, who say one thing and yet seem to believe something quite the opposite?

2. Is there any way of proving or disproving that God exists?

3. What do you find the hardest about believing there is a God?

4. What do you find the hardest about believing that there is no God?

_____

The Owl who was God

O nce upon a starless midnight, there was an owl who sat on the branch of an oak tree. Two ground moles tried to slip quietly by, unnoticed.

"You!" said the owl.

"Who?" they quavered, in fear and astonishment, for they could not believe it was possible for anyone to see them in that thick darkness.

"You two!" said the owl.

The moles hurried away and told the other creatures of the field and forest that the owl was the greatest and wisest of all animals because he could answer any question.

"I'll see about that," said the secretary bird, and he called on the owl one night when it was again very dark.

"How many claws am I holding up?" said the secretary bird.

"Two," said the owl, and that was right.

"Can you give me another expression for 'that is to say' or 'namely'?" asked the secretary bird.

"To wit," said the owl.

"Why does a lover call on his love?" asked the secretary bird.

"To woo," said the owl.

The secretary bird hastened back to the other creatures and reported that the owl was indeed the greatest and wisest animal in the world because he could see in the dark and because he could answer any question.

"Can he see in the daytime, too?" asked a red fox.

"Can he see in the daytime, too?" echoed a dormouse and a French poodle.

All the other creatures laughed loudly at this silly question, and they set upon the red fox and his friends and drove them out of the region. Then they sent a messenger to the owl and asked him to be their leader.

When the owl appeared among the animals, it was high noon and the sun was shining brightly. He walked very slowly, which gave him an appearance of great dignity, and he peered about him with large staring eyes, which gave him an air of tremendous importance.

"He's God!" screamed a Plymouth Rock hen. And the others took up the cry, "He's God!" So they followed him wherever he went and when he began to bump into things, they began to bump into things, too.

Finally, he came to a concrete highway and he started up the middle of it, and all the other creatures followed him. Presently, a hawk, who was acting as outrider, observed a truck coming towards them, and he reported to the secretary bird, and the secretary bird reported to the owl.

"There's danger ahead," said the secretary bird.

"To wit?" said the owl.

"Aren't you afraid?" asked the secretary bird.

"Who?" said the owl calmly, for he could not see the truck.

"He's God!" cried all the creatures again, and they were still crying 'He's God' when the truck hit them and ran them down. Some of the animals were merely injured, but most of them, including the owl, were killed.

▪ *Themes* ▪

Peer pressure – Independent thinking – Decision-making

▪ *For reflection and discussion* ▪

1. Which character is the most misguided in the story?

2. Who in the story should accept responsibility for what happened?

3. In what way do you experience the pressure to be like everyone else?

4. In what way can peer-group pressure benefit an individual?

The Quarreling
Sons

A man had four sons who always seemed to be bickering with each other. Nothing the father said made any difference to them and within a few hours, they would once again be arguing with each other. He was often telling them how much easier life would be if only they could learn to work together.

In his frustration one day, the father sent his sons out into the fields to find a piece of wood each. When the puzzled sons returned, the father tied the four sticks into a bundle and asked one of the sons to break it. The son tried his hardest to break the tightly bound bundle but he could not even bend the wood.

The father then untied the string and separated the sticks. "Now try," he said to the same boy while the others watched. The lad broke each stick with the greatest of ease. "Do you all see the point?" asked the father. "It is the same with you. If you stand together, nothing can defeat you; but as soon as you are divided, you become vulnerable."

▪ *Themes* ▪

Co-operation – Support – Unity

▪ *For reflection and discussion* ▪

1. How true is the statement: 'If you stand together, nothing can defeat you; but as soon as you are divided, you become vulnerable'?

2. Can you think of an event which was achieved only through the co-operation of many people?

3. Read I Corinthians 12:12–27. How does St. Paul argue for our need to be co-operative?

· *The Jester* ·

There is an old story of a jester who sometimes had very wise things to say. One day he said something so foolish that the King, handing him a staff, said to him, "Take this, and keep it till you find a bigger fool than yourself."

Some years later, the King was very ill and lay on his deathbed. His courtiers were called; his family and his servants also stood round his bedside. The King, addressing them, said, "I am about to leave you. I am going on a very long journey, and I shall not return again to this place, so I have called you all to say 'Goodbye'."

Then his jester stepped forward and, addressing the King, said, "Your Majesty, may I ask a question? When you journeyed abroad visiting your people, staying with your nobles, or paying diplomatic visits to other courts, your heralds and servants always went before you, making preparations for you. May I ask what preparations your Majesty has made for this long journey that he is about to take?"

"Alas!" replied the King, "I have made no preparations."

"Then," said the jester, "take this staff with you, for now I have found a bigger fool than myself."

· *Themes* ·

Readiness—Wisdom—Life after death

· *For reflection and discussion* ·

1. What 'preparations' do you think the court jester had in mind?

2. Read the Parable of the Ten Bridesmaids (Matthew 25:1–13). How would you define 'wisdom'? How would you define 'foolishness'?

3. Do you think that if the court jester lived among us today he would find many people deserving of his staff?

— ▪ *What is Bread?* ▪ —

A man was once brought before a jury of respectable and educated townsfolk to be tried for a crime he had allegedly committed. As the court began, the accused asked the judge how qualified the jurors were to judge him. "Are they experienced thinkers able to determine right from wrong?," he asked.

"I will show you how wise your jurors are," he continued.

"Please ask them to separately write an answer to my question: "What is bread?""

When the jury had finished, the answers were read:

The first juror said: "Bread is food."

The second: "It is a gift from the Almighty."

The third: "It is a mixture of flour, yeast and water."

The fourth said: "It is obvious it is baked dough."

The fifth: "It depends very much how you use the word 'bread'."

The sixth: "No one really knows."

The accused man looked the judge squarely in the face. "When the wise and educated decide what bread is," he said, "it may then be possible for them to determine what is right and wrong."

▪ *Themes* ▪

Justice–Wisdom–Right/Wrong

▪ *For reflection and discussion* ▪

1. Do you think the accused man has a fair point?

2. Are we prone to judging people and situations before we know the full story?

3. Read Matthew 7:1–5. What advice does this Scripture reading offer?

_____

— ▪ *The Chief Rabbi* ▪ —

Once upon a time, there was a chief Rabbi in the land who was so skilled that he could prevent any disaster from destroying his people. Once, when a war threatened them, they came to the Rabbi and begged him to call upon God to save them. The wise old man left his house and went to a secret place in the forest which only he knew. Once there, he built a special fire which only he knew how to build and when the fire was burning, he lifted up his hands and told God the whole story about the plight of his people. And God spared the people.

Well, as we all must, the old Rabbi died and his most capable student was chosen to succeed him as chief Rabbi. His successor was a wise and holy man, like himself, and the people had great trust in him. One day, however, a plague broke out and it looked as if the people would perish. So they came to the new Rabbi and begged him to call upon God to save them.

The Rabbi went to the sacred place in the forest, but when he got there he could only pound his fist on the ground because he had never learnt how to build the special fire. However, he lifted up his hands and told God the whole story anyway; and God spared his people.

Well, this Rabbi also died and his most capable student was just as wise and holy as all his predecessors, so the people had great trust in him, too.

But one year there was a great drought and there was great danger that the people would perish. They went in distress to the new Rabbi and begged him to call upon God to save them.

Well, this chief Rabbi not only did not know how to build the special fire, he had never even learnt where the secret place in the forest was! All he could do was lean back in his chair, throw up his hands, and tell God the whole story.

God spared the people from the drought, anyway, because, as you well know, the reason God created the human race was because . . . God loves stories.

▪ *Themes* ▪

Prayer–Ritual–Faith–Divine mercy

▪ *For reflection and discussion* ▪

1. Does God answer prayer?

2. Can God answer all prayers or only some prayers?

3. How important is it to know prayer formulas?

4. Read Matthew 6:5–15. What advice on prayer is offered in this passage?

— ▪ *The Oak Seedling* ▪ —

A small oak seedling was growing in the forest. It looked around and saw that some seedlings turned into great oak trees while others became no more than little shrubs. The trees were strong and beautiful. The shrubs were weak and ugly.

One day the forest ranger was passing through.

"Excuse me, Mr. Ranger, will you help me grow into a great tree?" the seedling asked.

"Do you really want that?" the ranger asked. "It will be a very painful process, one that will require great patience and incredible discipline. It is much easier to just be a shrub."

"No," the seedling replied, "I really want to be a great oak tree. I don't care what it costs in time and patience. I don't care how difficult it is. To be an oak tree is my only desire."

Every day when the ranger came the seedling's way, he poked at the soil, forced the seedling to stand straight and even pulled off some of his leaves and branches. Sometimes when other seedlings were close by, the ranger uprooted them and left the seedling all alone.

One day the seedling complained, "Why do you treat me so harshly? Why don't you let me do what I want to do? Why must you prune my branches, poke my soil, restrict my friends? Why can't you just let me be?"

The ranger replied, "There is only one way to be an oak tree. Because I want to help you, I must cause you some pain. That is the way of growth. Without pain you will be nothing more than a shrub, never a full grown tree."

▪ *Themes* ▪

Training–Formation–Discipline–Growth–Ambition–Pain

24

▪ *For reflection and discussion* ▪

1. Why is it easier to be 'just a shrub' rather than an oak tree?

2. Do you agree that sometimes parents must restrict the freedom of their children?

3. Read Paul's letter to the Ephesians 6:1–4. What advice does this reading offer to both parents and their children?

– ▪ *The Mustard Seed* ▪ –

There was once a woman whose only son died. In her grief, she went to a holy man and said, "What prayers, what magical incantations do you have to bring my son back to life?"

Instead of sending her away or reasoning with her, he said to her, "Fetch me a mustard seed from a home that has never known sorrow. We will use it to drive the sorrow out of your life."

The woman set off at once in search of that magical mustard seed. She came first to a splendid mansion, knocked at the door, and said, "I am looking for a home that has never known sorrow. Is this such a place? It is very important to me."

They told her, "You've certainly come to the wrong place," and began to describe all the tragic things that had recently befallen them.

The woman said to herself, "Who is better able to help these poor unfortunate people than I, who have had misfortune of my own?" She stayed to comfort them, then went on in her search for a home that had never known sorrow.

But wherever she turned, in hovels and in palaces, she found one tale after another of sadness and misfortune. Ultimately, she became so involved in ministering to other people's grief that she forgot about her quest for the magical mustard seed, never realizing that it had in fact driven the sorrow out of her life.

▪ *Themes* ▪

Grief – Bereavement – Ministry – Sorrow – Empathy

• *For reflection and discussion* •

1. Why was the woman sent out to find a mustard seed from a home that had never known sorrow?

2. What advice would you give to someone who suddenly finds him/herself alone?

3. Read 2 Corinthians 1:3–7. In what way does our suffering enable us to understand and sympathize with others?

_____

The Forgiving Stone

Two men once visited a holy man to ask his advice. "We have done wrong," they said, "and our consciences are troubled. Can you tell us what we must do so that we may be forgiven and feel clear of our guilt?"

"Tell me of your wrongdoings, my sons," said the old man.

The first man said, "I have committed a great and grievous sin."

"What about you?" the holy man asked the second.

"Oh," said he, "I have done quite a number of wrong things, but they are all quite small, and not at all important."

The holy man considered for a while. "This is what you must do," he said at last. "Each of you must go and bring me a stone for each of his misdeeds."

Off went the men, and presently the first came back, staggering with an enormous boulder, so heavy that he could hardly lift it, and with a groan he let it fall at the feet of the holy man. Then along came the second, cheerfully carrying a bag of small pebbles. This he also laid at the feet of the saint.

"Now," said the holy man, "take all those stones and put them back where you found them."

The first man shouldered his rock again, and staggered back to the place from which he had brought it. But the second man could only remember where a few of his pebbles had lain. After some time, he came back, and said that the task was too difficult.

"You must know, my son," said the old man, "that sins are like these stones. If a person has committed a great sin, it lies like a heavy stone on his or her conscience, but if there is true sorrow, there is forgiveness and the load is taken away. But if a person is constantly doing small things that are wrong, he or she does not feel any very great load of guilt, and therefore is not sorry, and remains a sinner. So, you see, it is as important to avoid little misdeeds as big ones."

▪ *Themes* ▪

Forgiveness—Reconciliation—Sin—Guilt

▪ *For reflection and discussion* ▪

1. What do you think the holy man was trying to say to his two visitors?

2. Do you agree with him?

3. If one commits no major sin, does that necessarily make one a 'good' person?

4. Think of some 'small' wrongdoings which can be destructive if they persist.

Parable of
• the Ant •

Once there was a colony of ants with only five legs. Whenever they walked, they went ONE-TWO-HITCH, ONE-TWO-HITCH, all along the path. These ants lived on decayed banana leaves and nothing else. I shouldn't say lived, for many of them died. Banana leaves, especially in their rotten state, are rather hard to find, and so the ants had a very hard life. Many of them died young from over-exertion and starvation.

Now, it happened one day that a very strange ant was born among them. This ant had six legs. All the ants clicked their tongues in consternation. Many tried their best to console the parents on their child's deformity. Some suggested that for the good of the community they ought to kill him in infancy, but the mother pleaded hard, so they let him live.

Strangely enough, this little ant was soon rushing around faster than his elders. And worse than that, he had a very awkward way of walking. "Look," they tried to tell him, "you don't know how to walk correctly. You have to go ONE-TWO-HITCH, ONE-TWO-HITCH. Now, try it properly."

So the little ant would try to put a little hitch in his step, but every time he tried, that sixth foot would come down and he'd leave his teachers far behind. They gave up in disgust. When he was half-grown, his elders noticed another peculiarity. He was eating breadcrumbs. "Stop," they cried. "They're poison. You mustn't do that. If you eat even two little pieces you'll die." But the little ant continued eating. They waited for him to fall over dead, but nothing happened. Instead, as the days went by, he grew strong and big, bigger even than the biggest of grownups. This was outrageous.

But the real crisis didn't come until he was fully grown.

The colony had been told to move quickly from their home to another place, for the dreaded driver ants were marching against them. The job of moving was very slow, for in order to move the nest, an egg had to be loaded on the back of an ant. Then two other ants climbed on his back, holding the egg in place. They had to keep it from rolling off at every hitch, you see. So the egg was carried along and the ant under the egg would be more dead than alive when they arrived.

They had just started moving their eggs when they noticed the six-legged monstrosity coming towards them at a rapid rate. "Hurry up, you lazy thing," they cried between puffs, "you have work to do." They had barely got the words out of their mouths when he passed them on the double and was back again carrying an egg between—of all places—his two front feet. "You can't do that," they screamed, "you'll break it. And anyway, you'll never get there."

"I've already been there and back twice," he replied, "and I haven't broken one yet. Let me show you how to do it."

This was the last straw. Almost choking with rage, they dropped their eggs in a heap and rushed at him. "He has a devil," cried his enemies. "He is perverting the peace. He is spoiling the nation. He is teaching others this treason. It is better that he should die than that our whole nation should perish. Away with him. Kill him."

"There," they growled in grim satisfaction some time later, "he'll never try to teach us again. We'll solve our own problems, thank you."

Then they went back to work.

ONE-TWO-HITCH,

    ONE-TWO-HITCH,

        ONE-TWO-HITCH ....

▪ *Themes* ▪

Prejudice—Discrimination—Persecution—Conformity—
Self-esteem—Assertiveness—Uniqueness

▪ *For reflection and discussion* ▪

1. What is the difference between 'uniformity' and 'conformity'?

2. Why do you think the ants did not appreciate being shown a different method of carrying food?

3. Read James 2:1–4. What does this reading say about our tendency to be prejudiced?

4. Do you think a 'Cut-down-the-tall-poppies' syndrome is evident here? What scriptural parallel comes to mind?

▬ • *The Tower* • ▬▬

There once was a country where none of the people ever lifted their heads. They always looked downwards, just in front of them. And yet every person in this country spent their whole life searching for the highest tower in the world.

Of course, no one ever found the tower, because not one head was lifted. And so they were a restless people, never happy with staying in one place, always searching and forever moving about. Every day you could see them walking up and down all the winding little roads, studying maps and arguing with each other.

There were, in fact, signs which pointed to the tower. But as the people wouldn't look up, they never saw the signs. Instead they argued with each other about the 'right' road to the tower. They never followed a road to its end, because as soon as they'd traveled a little way along it, they would be persuaded to try a different road. Thus they went round in circles.

One day a man named Trevor was walking about when he saw a large gathering of people. They were clustered around the lake, all pointing excitedly at the reflection of the tower in the water. Many of them jumped into the lake and were drowned. Some of the others said that the tower was evil; others said there was no tower.

In the commotion which followed, Trevor was knocked over. Now this might not sound like a very important event, but in a country where all the people always look down at the road in front of them—well, let's just say that people didn't fall over very often. When the crowd had cleared, Trevor was still lying flat on his back. But when he opened his eyes, he could see the tower, way off in the distance! He tried to tell his countrymen, but they thought he was mad. In fact, it was a sign of disgrace to have fallen over like that.

33

So Trevor journeyed towards the tower alone. There were many roads which seemed to lead to it, but he took the nearest one. The journey was not easy. The road was sometimes rough and bumpy. And he wasn't sure sometimes that he was heading in the right direction.

A couple of times he slipped and fell over. But it was at these times that he was able to gaze up at the tower and get his bearings once again.

And he noticed that the only other people who traveled in the right direction were the sick, the crippled, the lame and the hungry. For only they who had fallen were able to look up and see the tower.

▪ *Themes* ▪

Self-help – Disability – Search – Restlessness – Uniqueness – Persistence – Vision

▪ *For reflection and discussion* ▪

1. Why were the inhabitants of this country feeling restless? What causes restlessness?

2. Why did the sick, the disabled, and the underprivileged find it easier to journey towards the tower?

3. Read Luke 7:37–50. Why is it that the poor and rejected find God more quickly than the self-righteous and 'religious'?

4. Jean Vanier, modern-day apostle to the mentally handicapped, says that only those who recognize their own woundedness can help the needy. What do you think of this 'wounded healer' idea?

▪ *The Race* ▪

Three people lived in the same street close to each other. Their names were John, Paula and Jacob. They lived in comfortable houses in a comfortable street with nice lawns and they thought well of one another. Then one day John thought he saw Paula looking enviously at his rose garden with its rare blooms, so he bought an air rifle, and slept with it under his pillow. Jacob heard about this, so he also bought an air rifle — to protect his property. Before long everyone in the street had one too.

Paula realized she was the only one who didn't have a rifle, so she bought herself one the first chance she had. John thought he had better keep one step ahead of the others, so he traded in his air rifle for a double-barreled shotgun, and had the locks on his door changed one morning after church. Paula and Jacob heard about this, and quickly did the same. Then Jacob didn't like the way John and Paula and the others could see into his yard, so he had a six foot timber fence put around it, and he and his family kept watch night and day.

When John saw this, he too had a six foot fence built around his property with barbed wire at the top. Paula went one better — she had her barbed wire electrified. Jacob was a little worried now because the others were ahead of him . . . so as well as the electrified barbed wire he bought a few dozen hand grenades — just in case. He had heard that someone down the road had flame throwers but he was not sure.

In the dead of night, when they thought no one could see them, John and Paula went to two different weapon stores to buy supplies of something a little more powerful. John bought napalm while Paula was interested in the poisonous chemicals and germs which could be sprayed in a gas. Jacob saw what was going on but he did not worry about buying supplies at the weapon stores; he was experimenting in his basement with something called "nuclear".

Meanwhile, their houses were being neglected, they did not have enough money to buy clothes and food for their families, their gardens were overrun with weeds, it was too dangerous to let the children play in the park, and there was no time to just enjoy life any more.

▪ *Themes* ▪

Nuclear threat–Weapons–Paranoia–Envy–Security–Militarism–Arms race

▪ *For reflection and discussion* ▪

1. Why is this story entitled: 'The Race'? Of what does it remind you?

2. What underlying emotion led all the people in the street to buy more and more weapons?

3. If you lived in this street, what could you do?

4. Read Ephesians 2:14–22. How does Jesus Christ bring about peace in the world?

— ▪ *Bad Strategy* ▪ —

There was once a farmer who owned a goose that could lay golden eggs. Every night the goose was given a bowl of the best corn and every morning the farmer and his wife would find a solid gold egg in the pen.

One morning the farmer's wife said, "We are fortunate indeed to own such a clever goose. We will be rich one day, but it is going to take such a very long time. We may even be too old to enjoy it!"

The farmer thought about this for some time and he eventually came up with an idea. He went to his wife and said: "It is clear the goose must have a store of eggs inside her. Why should we wait all our lives while she lays them one by one? Get me the knife and we'll have all the gold at once."

The wife was a little doubtful about treating the goose in this way, but on the other hand, becoming instantly rich had its advantages.

The goose was killed and cut open and, to their great dismay, it was no different from any other goose. "We'll not get rich quickly or slowly now," said the farmer quietly.

▪ *Themes* ▪

Impatience – Greed – Wealth

▪ *For reflection and discussion* ▪

1. It is often said that 'patience is a virtue'. Do you agree?

2. What are some of life's riches that cannot be hurried?

3. Discuss the following definition of 'patience':

The grace which enables us to bear afflictions and calamities with constancy and calmness of mind, and with a ready submission to the will of God.

The Discarded Chair

There once was a chair that was never used or sat upon because it had become so old and decrepit. It was shoved into a corner, and now and then the people who lived in the house would look at it and say, "One day soon we must take that old chair and throw it into the dump."

When they said that, the old chair would shudder and feel more frail than it really was. But the thing that bothered the chair most of all was that when friends would gather for parties and conversation in the home, all the other chairs were used. Indeed, the people would sit on the floor rather than touch the old worn-out chair in the corner.

One night, when the old chair was in the deepest kind of depression because it was unnoticed, untouched, unused and unwanted, a strange-looking creature entered through a tiny hole in the floor, looked this way and that, and approached the old chair in the corner. It said, "My, you look so sad and lonely, old chair. Hasn't anyone sat in you lately?" (Obviously you must know that this tiny creature was a 'Homer', for the Homer is the only one of God's creatures who can communicate with a chair.)

"Oh, you don't know how glad I am to see you," sobbed the old chair. "The other chairs won't have anything to do with me, and no Homer has passed this way in years."

"I understand," replied the Homer. "As a matter of fact the Lord Homer asked me to stop by because he sensed you were in a terrible state."

"What can you do to help me?" exclaimed the chair. "Some might find me valuable as an antique, but folks here just see me as a wobbly, unsightly old chair."

"Count on me," said the Homer. "You need to be found by

someone who appreciates all you have to give." And with that he disappeared suddenly through the hole in the floor.

The man in the yellow muffler, who stopped by the house the next day to ring the door bell, was puzzled at how he could have ever lost his way. He never realized that while he was driving his car, a Homer had slipped in at the service station when he stopped for gas. Homers, of course, have the power to lead you to one home or another.

"I've lost my way," said the man to the lady of the house. And then he spied the old chair. "Why, you have what I've been looking for," he cried. "Would you sell that chair to me?"

"That old chair!" said the surprised woman. "Is it valuable? We were going to throw it away."

"Valuable to me," answered the man in the yellow muffler.

"If it is that valuable, I'd rather not sell it but fix it up myself," thought the woman.

And that is why the old chair was refinished and repaired. Indeed, it became the central object of furniture in the entire house. "See this chair?" the lady would tell her friends. "It's the most precious object in our house."

▪ *Themes* ▪

Old age – Home – Appreciation – Re-evaluation – Affirmation –
Loneliness – Self-esteem

▪ *For reflection and discussion* ▪

1. In what ways do we sometimes discard people?

2. Why do you think the imaginary 'Homer' was sent to speak with the chair?

3. Read Matthew 10:29–31. What does this reading say about the value of each person before God?

_____

Parable of the
Unknown God

Upon a mountain top there lived a kind and gentle God. In the village far below, his people lived. They were a very busy people, with many books to read and many games to play, and very many meetings to attend. They seldom thought about the kind and gentle God, so far away he seemed. No one had ever seen his face. Some doubted he was even there at all.

Yet, day by day the gentle God looked down upon his own, and wanted very much that they should be his friends. "I must," he thought, "do some small thing to show them that I care." And so, each day, he sent a messenger to the village, a pack upon his back, and in the pack he bore a special gift, a gift for every person in the land.

Each day the gifts would come. Each day the people ran with open arms to gather them. But soon they grew quite used to being gifted. Some began to grab gifts from the pack, and some took more than they were meant to have, and some complained of gifts that were too small. At last no one remembered from where the gifts had come. And no one even thought to ask.

Far up on his mountain top sat God. Day after lonely day he waited for a friendly word, a sign of thanks, or just a "Hi, God. I know you're there."

But no word came. The people took the gifts as if they had a right to them, and more. God? Well, he was far away. And some said, "What's he ever done for me?" And some, "I don't believe he even *is*."

"If I can't tell them that I am," God thought, "how can I tell them that I am a friend, and want to give them friendship most of all?"

And then his eyes lit up. "I know," he said, "I'll give a party for my friends below. I'll give a party and invite them all. And surely if they spend some time with me, and learn to know how much I really care, oh, surely then they'll come to know I am their friend."

And so the invitations were sent out. A list was posted on the town house wall for all who wished to come to sign their names.

The people saw the invitation. Some just laughed and said, "That's not for me!" And some said, "Spend a day with God? No way!" And some were very busy with their chores and said, "Some other time but not today." And some were tempted: "Maybe it's for real, and maybe God does want to be my friend." And timidly they signed up for the day. But when the others laughed, they were ashamed and found excuses why they couldn't go.

The party day arrived, but no one went. And in his mountain home the kind God sat. "I only want to give them love," he said. "How can I tell them? Make them understand? Is there no one who wants me for a friend?"

And in the village far below, the people laughed and cried and worked and played and died. And seldom thought about the gentle God who loved them very much.

▪ *Themes* ▪

Ingratitude – Giftedness – Doubt – Celebration – Friendship – God – Peer pressure

▪ *For reflection and discussion* ▪

1. Why did the people not realize from where the gifts were coming?

2. What do you think are the main gifts that God grants his people?

3. Read John 10:7–16. Explain what Jesus means when he says, 'I have come in order that you might have life—Life in all its fullness.'

─ ▪ *The Stonecutter* ▪ ─

This is the story of Nashti, a poor Japanese stonecutter who lived in a tiny hut on the outskirts of a village. One day as Nashti was working with his hammer and chisel upon a huge stone, he heard the crowd gathering along the streets to watch the King go by. Joining the crowd, the stonecutter gazed in awe as the King, dressed in marvelous clothing, was greeted by his subjects.

"Oh, how I wish I had the power and glory and finery of the King," he thought. "He has the whole world at his command. There is no one more powerful than the King."

His thoughts were heard in the heavens, and immediately the humble Nashti was transformed into a powerful King. He found himself riding on a great horse, waving at the crowds of people who had flocked to see him. "This is power!" he exulted.

As the summer progressed, however, the new King watched the effects of the heat upon his people. Men and animals became weary, and plants withered under the powerful rays of the sun. As he looked at the sky, the new King realized that the sun was far more powerful than he was. He thought, "I wish I were the sun." Immediately his wish was granted.

How the stonecutter relished his new role as the sun! He gloried in the power he felt as he surveyed the kingdoms below him. As he sent his bright rays to the earth, he watched kings and princes hide under his gaze. Even the crops in the field were under his command.

Then one day a tiny cloud moved over the land, shielding the earth from the sun's bright rays. Seeing that here was something more powerful, Nashti thought, "I want very much to be a cloud." Again, his wish was granted.

Now he blocked the sun's rays and felt important. He gathered all of his strength, becoming a gigantic cloud, and began to pour down rain on the earth. Rivers formed where previously there were none, and water flooded the streets of the cities and the farmland. Everything—trees, animals, people—seemed to be awed by his power. Everything except a huge rock that remained untouched. Again he had discovered something more powerful. "There is nothing," he thought, "as powerful as a rock. How I wish I were a huge stone!" His wish was granted.

As a stone he remained motionless and powerful, unmoved by either sun or rain or anything that nature could bring. Nashti felt exempt from all the forces that shaped the life and existence of those around him.

Then one day a man approached him, carrying a bag. When he stopped, he pulled out a chisel and a hammer and began to chip away at the rock. Realizing that the man with the tools was more powerful than any rock, he cried out, "Oh, I want to be a stonecutter."

Once again the heavens heard his cry and he became a stonecutter. Once again he lived in a tiny hut and made his living with hammer and chisel.

▪ *Themes* ▪

Self-acceptance–Power–Prayer–Discontent

▪ *For reflection and discussion* ▪

1. What do you think led Nashti to wish to be someone else?

2. Do you know people who keep changing jobs and locations and never seem content where they are?

3. Read Matthew 5:3–12. How do the Beatitudes define happiness?

_____

What Happened
to Charles

A farm horse named Charles was led to town one day by his owner, to be shod. He would have been shod and brought back home without incident if it hadn't been for Eva, a duck, who was always hanging about the kitchen door of the farmhouse, eavesdropping, and never got anything quite right. Her farm-mates said of her that she had two mouths but only one ear.

On the day that Charles was led away to the smithy, Eva went quacking about the farm, excitedly telling the other animals that Charles had been taken to town to be shot.

"They're executing an innocent horse!" cried Eva. "He's a hero! He's a martyr! He died to make us free!"

"He was the greatest horse in the world," sobbed a sentimental hen.

"He just seemed like old Charley to me," said a realistic cow. "Let's not get into a moony mood."

"He was wonderful!" cried a gullible goose.

"What did he ever do?" asked a goat.

Eva, who was as inventive as she was inaccurate, turned on her lively imagination. "It was butchers who led him off to be shot!" she shrieked. "They would have cut our throats while we slept if it hadn't been for Charles!"

"I didn't see any butchers, and I can see a burnt-out firefly on a moonless night," said a barn owl. "I didn't hear any butchers, and I can hear a mouse walk across moss."

"We must build a memorial to Charles the Great, who saved our lives," quacked Eva. And all the birds and beasts in the barnyard except the wise owl, the skeptical goat, and the realistic cow set about building a memorial.

Just then the farmer appeared in the lane, leading Charles, whose new shoes glinted in the sunlight.

It was lucky that Charles was not alone, for the memorial-builders might have set upon him with clubs and stones for replacing their hero with just plain old Charlie. It was lucky, too, that they could not reach the barn owl, who quickly perched upon the weathervane of the barn, for none is so exasperating as he who is right! The sentimental hen and the gullible goose were the ones who finally called attention to the true culprit—Eva, the one-eared duck with two mouths. The others set upon her and tarred and unfeathered her, for none is more unpopular than the bearer of sad tidings that turn out to be false.

▪ *Themes* ▪

Gullibility–Gossip–Imagination–Wisdom–Prayer–Faith

▪ *For reflection and discussion* ▪

1. What was the main cause of the whole ridiculous chain of events?

2. If a similar situation occurred in real life, which character would you most resemble? Why?

3. In your experience, is it possible, without even trying, to find yourself suddenly being praised and appreciated?

4. Read: James 3:1–12. What warnings does the writer give on the misuse of one's tongue?

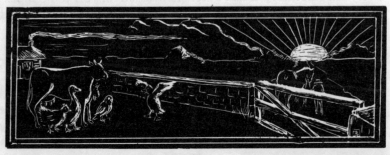

The Canoe,
the Boat and
the Helicopter

Prolonged torrential rain high up in the mountains caused the river to burst its banks and flood the plain. Roads became impassable, and soon villages and towns were in danger of being swept away. All sorts of emergency services were rushed in to help as a massive rescue operation was launched.

The minister of one of the churches had sought refuge at the top of one of his apple trees, and there he prayed to God for help as the water crept higher and higher. As he sat crouched on the top-most branch, a young lad came paddling by in a tiny canoe. When he saw the minister crouched in the apple tree, he paddled towards him and said, "Would you like a lift? You can squeeze into the space in front of me if you like."

The minister thanked the boy, and said, "No, thank you, I will be all right. I have faith in God."

A few minutes later a boat full of survivors floated into view. When they saw the minister, they 'hove to' and offered him a lift to higher ground. But the minister declined, preferring to put his trust in God.

Finally a helicopter flew by. Hovering over the tree, the crewman lowered a rope ladder and signaled to the minister to climb up. But once again, the minister declined the offer.

"No thanks," he shouted, "I have faith in God, and He will save me!"

So the helicopter flew away. The waters continued to rise and the minister, who could not swim, was drowned.

Soon afterwards, he found himself in heaven, standing before the throne of God.

"Tell me, Lord," he said, with a certain reproach in his voice, "why didn't you save me from drowning? I thought you not only looked after, but also listened to the prayers of those who put their trust in you."

God replied, "I always look after my children and I always listen to their prayers. What more could I have done for you? I sent a canoe, a boat and a helicopter, but you turned them all away."

▪ *Themes* ▪

Prayer—Faith

▪ *For reflection and discussion* ▪

1. What is the lesson the minister learns when he questions God in heaven?

2. Recall or imagine another crisis situation in which an attitude like the minister's is evident.

3. Read Matthew 7:7–11. What is the advice St. Matthew offers us?

— · *The Last Flower* · —

World War XII, as everybody knows, brought about the collapse of civilization. Towns, cities and villages disappeared from the earth. All the groves and forests were destroyed, and all the gardens and all the works of art. Men, women and children became lower than the lower animals. Discouraged and disillusioned, dogs deserted their fallen masters.

Emboldened by the pitiful condition of the former lords of the earth, rabbits descended upon them. Books, paintings and music disappeared from the earth, and human beings just sat around, doing nothing. Years and years went by. Even the few generals who were left forgot what the last war had decided. Boys and girls grew up to stare at each other blankly, for love had passed from the earth.

One day a young girl who had never seen a flower chanced to come upon the last one in the world. She told the other human beings that the last flower was dying. The only one who paid any attention to her was a young man she found wandering about. Together the young man and the girl nurtured the flower and it began to live again.

One day a bee visited the flower, and a hummingbird. Before long there were two flowers, and then four and then a great many. Groves and forests flourished again and the young girl began to take an interest in how she looked. The young man discovered that touching the girl was pleasurable.

Love was reborn into the world. Their children grew up strong and healthy and learned to run and laugh. Dogs came out of their exile.

The young man discovered, by putting one stone upon another, how to build a shelter. Soon everybody was building shelters. Towers, cities and villages sprang up. Song came back into the world and troubadours and jugglers and tailors and cobblers and painters and poets and sculptors and wheelwrights and soldiers and lieutenants and captains and generals and major-generals and liberators.

Some people went to one place to live, and some to another. Before long, those who went to live in the valleys wished they had gone to live in the hills and those who had gone to live in the hills wished they had gone to live in the valleys.

The liberators, under the guidance of God, set fire to the discontent. So presently the world was at war again. This time, the destruction was so complete . . . that nothing at all was left in the world except one man and one woman and one flower.

▪ *Themes* ▪

Arms race – Environment – War – Love – Relationships – Peace

▪ *For reflection and discussion* ▪

1. How do you think World War XII brought about the collapse of civilization?

2. Why do you think the flower attracted the young girl?

3. Why did people begin to fight again? Does that sound true to life?

4. Can you suggest a strategy which would help achieve world peace?

A Story of
■ *Fieldmice* ■

Once upon a time, in a field not very far from here, there lived a little village of fieldmice. They were very happy and led a quiet and peaceful life. They liked being with one another and helping each other. No one was ever lonely or hungry or needed a friend. They used to sing beautiful songs together and dance beautiful dances. No one ever heard them fighting.

Then, one day, a rather strange and tubby fieldmouse appeared. He had a big curly moustache, smoked a long cigar and had watery eyes behind an enormous pair of sunglasses. You knew they must be watery because he kept dabbing them with a huge purple and orange handkerchief which he kept in a pocket of his little waistcoat.

He spoke to the tiny fieldmice in a big oily voice and told them that they didn't really know how to enjoy life. He said to them, "You should have a mardi gras and really learn to celebrate." The fieldmice were even more puzzled. What could a mardi gras be all about?

Guessing that they were a little confused, the big city mouse with the moustache and the cigar and the watery eyes behind the sunglasses, told them that the mardi gras was a big celebration. "Everywhere in the city there are streamers and balloons, and all the mice put great big colored masks on their faces and paint their tails bright colors, and they all join in a great procession with singing and dancing and lots of tambourines playing. After the procession, they all go about frightening each other in their different masks, and the one with the most frightening mask wins the grand prize."

Some of the little fieldmice weren't too sure about this and so they argued a bit, but they finally decided that they might as well go ahead and have a mardi gras themselves. Almost before you knew it, the field where they lived became the most colorful sight you ever saw! They tore down branches and painted them, they tore up bunches of grass and made streamers from them and, for their masks, they took the bark off trees and made some of the most fierce-looking masks you could ever imagine! Some even painted their tails.

They had their procession and a fine affair it was, too, with singing and dancing and all, just as the city mice had it, but it wasn't long at all before they started frightening each other with their masks and some got really frightened. Just so no one would know who had been the meanest, they all decided to keep their masks on and keep frightening one another and, before long, they had forgotten how to get their masks off and how to get the paint off their tails.

One little mouse, with a bright green tail, scrubbed and scrubbed and scrubbed, but nothing came off, and she fainted from all the effort.

Eventually the fieldmice started fighting one another, and frightening each other worse than ever, and no one was brave enough to take his or her mask off and put an end to the fighting. Of course, by this time, all the streamers had blown away, and the field was a very ugly place. And, of course, the big tubby mouse from the city, with the big moustache and the eyes that watered all the time from the smoke of his cigar, had gone far, far away.

The poor fieldmice forgot what life had been like before the city mouse came, before they had settled down to fighting.

Then, one day, a very quiet mouse came. He was tall and handsome, with a beautiful look in his eyes. He began speaking to the fieldmice, who were so tired from fighting that they just sat and listened. He explained to them that if they really wanted to, they could take off all those masks and stop fighting and hurting each other. All they had to do was say "sorry" and they would find it easy to take the masks away.

Once one of the mice got brave enough, he said, "Sorry," to the mouse he had just been punching, and took off his mask — and ever so slowly all the mice began to take off their masks. You should have seen their faces as they saw each other again, and began to remember what life could really be like if they loved each other once more.

After a while, every last mask was off and all were being burnt in a huge bonfire. While the masks were burning, the fieldmice were hugging each other with happy tears running down their faces, and were dancing together around the fire. They were so happy that they danced all night and all the next day, and as they danced, they sang, filling the air with music.

▪ *Themes* ▪

Music–Forgiveness–Reconciliation–Celebration–
Communication–Masks–Relationships–Love

▪ *For reflection and discussion* ▪

1. What was the result of the mardi gras?

2. In what ways do we sometimes hide behind masks?

3. Why did it take an outsider, the gentle, tall mouse, to start the process of change?

4. Read Luke 6:37–42. To what extent will God forgive us?

— • *The Poor Beggar* • —

There is a fable well known in India of a poor beggar who lived in a State ruled by a Maharaja. The beggar had no home but put up every night in a free lodging-house, sleeping on a mat on the floor, and covering himself in the cooler nights with old rags. Having no means of earning a livelihood other than begging, he used to go out in the morning after a meal of cold rice left over from the previous day and sit by the wayside with his beggar's bowl. Passers-by used to throw some grains of rice or copper coins his way, so he usually had enough rice for two meals a day, and enough money to buy sticks for a fire and a few vegetables, fish or dhall for curry.

One day he heard that on the morrow, the Maharaja himself was coming that way in his chariot. That raised his hopes, for he said to himself, "The Maharaja will not give me a handful of rice or a copper coin, but nothing less than gold." The next day he took up his usual position by the side of the road, and patiently awaited the Maharaja's coming. The sun stood overhead and still he waited in the noonday heat, but no sign of the ruler. Patiently he waited, still full of hope, until almost sunset, and then he heard the welcome sound of the horses' hoofs and the chariot wheels.

Stepping into the road, he brought the chariot to a standstill, approached the Maharaja and begged for alms. Instead of giving him anything, the Maharaja extended his hands and asked the beggar to give *him* something.

Extremely disappointed and disgusted at a wealthy ruler begging from a poor beggar, he counted out five grains of rice from his bowl and placed them angrily in the hands of the Maharaja. "Thank you," said the Maharaja, and continued his journey.

With a sore heart, the beggar went that evening to his lodging house, took out his winnowing fan and began to clean his rice for his meal. As he did so, a small glittering object attracted his attention. Picking it up, he saw that it was a grain of gold. Laying it carefully to one side, he went on winnowing till he found another glittering golden grain, then another.

Now the search began in real earnest, and a fourth was found among the rice. After another search he saw a fifth and put it with the others. But no matter how long he searched after that, he found not another grain of gold.

Then the truth dawned on him. Five grains of rice given to the Maharaja had brought him in return five grains of gold. "What a fool I was!" he exclaimed regretfully. "If I'd known, I'd have given it all to him."

▪ *Themes* ▪

Poverty–Generosity–Sharing–Giving

▪ *For reflection and discussion* ▪

1. An Aboriginal speaker was asked at a conference: 'What can white Christians learn from Aboriginal spirituality and values?' He replied: 'How to share.' What do you think he would say about this story?

2. Is it true that we gain more from giving than receiving?

3. Read 2 Corinthians 8:1–15. Why does St. Paul insist that as Christians, we should learn to share?

A Story of
Growth

An old teacher was once taking a walk through a forest with a pupil by his side. The old man suddenly stopped and pointed to four plants close by his side. The first was just beginning to peep above the ground, the second had rooted itself pretty well into the earth, the third was a small shrub, while the fourth was a full-sized tree.

The tutor said to his young companion, "Pull up the first." The boy easily pulled it up with his fingers. "Now pull up the second." The youth obeyed, but found the task not so easy. "Now the third." The boy had to put forth all his strength, and was obliged to use both arms to uproot it.

"And now," said the master, "try your hand at the fourth." But the trunk of the tall tree, grasped in the arms of the youth, hardly shook its leaves.

"This, my son, is just what happens with our bad habits. When they are young, we can cast them out more readily with the help of God; but when they are old, it is hard to uproot them, though we pray and struggle ever so sincerely."

▪ Themes ▪

Habits–Addictions–Personal development

▪ For reflection and discussion ▪

1. Comment on the meaning of the word, 'growth' in the title of this story—if bad habits grow strong, what other growth is affected?

2. What are some 'bad habits' which easily become entrenched if not dealt with early?

3. Read James 1:19–26; 1:3; 11–16. To which bad habits do these readings refer?

_____

The Sound
of the Song

Once there was a village where the people had never heard music. They spoke to each other very loudly, even to the point of shouting. Because they tried so hard to have their own words heard, they weren't able to hear each other's words. This only made them shout all the louder in an attempt to be heard. The village became increasingly noisy.

There were three men in that village who could not speak, for they were dumb. They weren't able to communicate with the other people in the village, so no one really bothered with them. They used to meet together down by a little nearby brook. The bubbling sound of the brook seemed to make them happy.

One day, they realized why the brook made them feel so happy—it was because it was speaking to them, in a special way, without words and without shouting. The bubbling sounds of the little brook made music, which touched their souls.

So the men began to hum in tune with the music of the brook. At once they knew that they were communicating with each other. They were so excited that they ran into the noisy village, humming their tune. The people of the village marveled and fell silent, for they had never heard music before.

At that very moment, something even more wonderful happened. From over the hill came the sound of a powerful voice; not a voice of shouting, but one whose words filled the silence with song. No one knew whose voice it was, but it was beautiful. And as the three dumb men continued to hum, one by one the people of the village began to sing. The words they sang were not all the same, nor were the voices, but the tune blended them all together into a magnificent chorus of song.

And so the village became noisy again, only this time with the sound of song instead of shouting. And this time everyone listened.

▪ *Themes* ▪

Communication–Music–Noise pollution–Harmony–
Listening

▪ *For reflection and discussion* ▪

1. To what extent is it true that in trying to have our own words heard, we are unable to hear each other's words?

2. Why do you think that communication is often referred to as an 'art'?

3. Read Ephesians 4:29. How do we learn not to use 'harmful' words, but only helpful ones?

The Quails and
the Hunter

Once upon a time, a flock of quail lived near a marsh and they would fly to the nearby fields every day to feed. The only problem was that there was a Bird Hunter who lived nearby, and of late he had gotten to snare many quail in his net to take them to a nearby market to be sold. The reason he had grown so successful in catching them was that he had learned to imitate perfectly the call of the Leader. The Bird Hunter gave the call, and the quail, thinking it was the Leader, flew to his area where he tossed his net over them and captured them.

One day, the Leader called all the quails together for a conference. He said, "We are becoming decimated! Soon there will be none of us left. The Bird Hunter is catching us all. But I have found out how he does it. He learned my call and deceives you!

"But I have a plan. The next time you hear what you think is my call and fly to the area and the Bird Hunter throws his net on top of you, here is what you are to do: all together, you stick your heads through the openings in the net, and in one motion fly up with the net and land on the thorn bush. The net will stick there, you extricate yourselves, and the Bird Hunter will have to spend all day freeing his net."

And this is what they did. The Bird Hunter came, gave the imitation call, and the quail came. When the net was thrown over them, as one body they stuck their heads through the openings, and flew away to the thorn bush. They left a frustrated Hunter trying all day to get his net loose.

This went on for some time until the Hunter's wife bitterly complained that her husband was bringing home no quail to bring to market. They were becoming poor. The Bird Hunter listened to his wife, told her of the actions of the quail, and with his hand on his chin, added, "But, be patient, dear wife. Just wait till they quarrel. Then we shall catch them again."

Well, it so happened that one day when the Bird Hunter made his call, all the quail rose up and flew to the area where he was. But as they were landing, one quail accidentally brushed against another. "Will you watch where you're going, you clumsy ox!" cried the one quail.

The other said hastily, "Oh, I'm sorry, I really am. I didn't mean to do it. It was an accident."

"An accident, was it," cried the first quail. "If you'd watch where you're going instead of peering all about, you wouldn't be so clumsy."

"Well," said the second quail, "I don't know why you take that attitude. I said I was sorry, and if you can't accept that . . ." And they got to quarreling. Soon the others, perceiving the argument, gathered around and took sides, one for the first quail and the other for the second.

Meanwhile, the Bird Hunter had his net ready and threw it over the birds. They began to cry to one another, "Come, let us stop arguing and hurry or else we'll be caught. Let's fly over that way!"

But the other quail responded, "No, we're always flying over that way. We're always doing what you people want. Come, let us fly this way!" And while they were arguing which way to go, the Bird Hunter, with a smile on his face, gathered them up in the net, brought them to market, and that day made a fine penny.

▪ *Themes* ▪

Quarreling—Unity—Co-operation

▪ *For reflection and discussion* ▪

1. Why did the Hunter assume that eventually he would catch the quails?

2. Did you think it unrealistic that all the trouble started when one quail accidentally brushed against another?

3. Can you give examples of achievements for which co-operation is absolutely essential?

_____

The Farming Town

————— ▪ ————— ▪ —————

Once there was a farming town that could be reached only by a narrow road with a bad curve in it. There were frequent accidents on the road, especially at the curve, and the preacher would preach to the people of the town to make sure they were Good Samaritans. And they were. After each accident they would attend to the victims, for this was a religious work.

One day someone suggested they buy an ambulance to get the accident victims to the town hospital more quickly. The preacher preached and the people gave, for this was a religious work.

Then some time later, a councilman suggested that the town authorize the building of a wider road and the removal of the dangerous curve. Now it happened that the mayor had a farm market right at the curve on the road and he was against taking out the curve. Someone asked the preacher to say a word to the mayor and the congregation next Sunday about it. But the preacher and most of the people figured they had better stay out of politics.

So on the next Sunday the preacher preached on the Good Samaritan Gospel and encouraged the people to continue their fine work of picking up the accident victims — which they did. For this was a religious work.

▪ *Themes* ▪

Preventive care – Responsibility – Religion – Works – Injustice –
Conflict of interest – Politics and religion

▪ *For reflection and discussion* ▪

1. Does our Christian responsibility go beyond simply picking up the victims of injustice?

2. Some people define 'religious works' in a narrow sense. Others give the term a much broader meaning. Try writing your own definition and then decide whether it fits into the narrow or the broad category.

3. The world-famous champion of the poor, Archbishop Helder Camara, once said: 'When I give food to the poor, they call me a saint. When I ask why the poor have no food, they call me a communist.' Reflect on his comment in the light of this story.

Tale of a
Bad Man

Once, a very bad man died and went before the judgment throne. Before him stood Abraham, David, Peter, and Luke. A chilly silence hung heavy in the room as an unseen voice began to read the details of the man's life. There was nothing good that was recorded. When the voice concluded, Abraham spoke: "Men like you cannot enter the heavenly kingdom. You must leave."

"Father Abraham," the man cried, "I do not defend myself. I have no choice but to ask for mercy. Certainly you understand. Though you lied to save your own life, saying your wife was your sister, by the grace and mercy of God you became a blessing to all nations."

David interrupted, "Abraham has spoken correctly. You have committed evil and heinous crimes. You do not belong in the kingdom of light."

The man faced the great king and cried, "Son of Jesse, it is true. I am a wicked man. Yet I dare ask you for forgiveness. You slept with Uriah's wife and later, to cover your sin, arranged his death. I ask only forgiveness as you have known it."

Peter was next to speak. "Unlike David, you have shown no love to God. By your acid tongue and your vile temper, you have wounded the Son of God."

"I should be silent," the man muttered. "The only way I have used the blessed name of Jesus is in anger. Still, Simon, Son of John, I plead for grace. Though you walked by his side and listened to words from his lips, you slept when he needed you in the garden, and you denied him three times in his night of greatest need."

Then Luke the evangelist spoke, "You must leave. You have not been found worthy of the Kingdom of God."

The man's head bowed sadly for a moment before a spark lit in his face. "My life has been recorded correctly," the man began slowly. "I am guilty as charged. Yet I know there is a place for me in this blessed kingdom. Abraham, David, and Peter will plead my cause because they know of the weakness of man and the mercy of God. You, blessed physician, will open the gates to me because you have written of God's great love for the likes of me. Don't you recognize me? I am the lost sheep that the Good Shepherd carried home. I am your younger, prodigal brother."

And the gates opened and Luke embraced the sinner.

▪ *Themes* ▪

Acceptance–Mercy–Forgiveness–Guilt

▪ *For reflection and discussion* ▪

1. On what basis did the 'bad man' appeal for mercy to Abraham, David and Peter?

2. What other biblical examples can you give of good people who did not always do the right thing?

3. Read Luke 15:1–7; 11–24. What do these readings say about the nature of God's forgiveness?

▪ *Genesis* ▪

"Who are you?" said the Prime Minister, opening the door.

"I am God," replied the stranger.

"I don't believe you," sneered the Prime Minister. "Show me a miracle." And God showed the Prime Minister the miracle of birth.

"Pah!" said the Prime Minister. "My scientists are creating life in test-tubes and have nearly solved the secret of heredity. Artificial insemination is more certain than your lackadaisical method, and by cross-breeding we are producing fish and mammals to our design. Show me a proper miracle."

And God caused the sky to darken and hailstones came pouring down. "That's nothing," said the Prime Minister, picking up the telephone to the Air Ministry. "Send up a met plane, would you, and sprinkle the clouds with silver chloride crystals."

And the met plane went up and sprinkled the clouds which had darkened the world and the hailstones stopped pouring down and the sun shone brightly.

"Show me another," said the Prime Minister.

And God caused a plague of frogs to descend upon the land.

The Prime Minister picked up his telephone. "Get the Ministry for the environment," he said to the operator, "and instruct them to develop a frog-killer virus."

And soon the land was free of frogs, and the people gave thanks to the Prime Minister and erected laboratories in his name.

"Show me another," sneered the Prime Minister.

And God caused the sea to divide.

"Paltry tricks," said the Prime Minister as he picked up his direct-link-telephone to the Polaris submarine. "Lob a few missiles into Antarctica and melt the ice-cap, please."

And the ice-cap melted into water and the sea came rushing back.

"I control matters of life and death," said God.

"Do you?" said the Prime Minister. "Watch this." He pressed a button on his desk. And missiles flew to their pre-ordained destinations and H-bombs split the world asunder and radio-activity killed every mortal thing.

"I can raise the dead," said God.

"Please," said the Prime Minister in his cardboard coffin. "Let me live again."

"Why, who are you?" said God, closing the lid.

▪ *Themes* ▪

Technology–Genetic engineering–Environment–Miracles–
Skepticism–Power

▪ *For reflection and discussion* ▪

1. How did you react to the ending of this story? Would you want to re-write it?

2. What does this story imply about trying to convince skeptics of God's role?

3. What examples do we have in our world of the 'grandeur of God'?

4. Read I Corinthians: 1:18–31. What does St. Paul mean when he says: 'No one can boast in God's presence'?

The Hermit and
the Three Robbers

A certain hermit was walking one day in a deserted place when he came across an enormous cave, the entrance to which was not easily visible. He decided to rest inside, and entered. Soon, however, he noticed the bright reflection of the light upon a large quantity of gold within.

As soon as he became aware of what he had seen, the hermit took to his heels and fled as fast as he could.

Now in this desert area were three robbers, who spent much of their time there so that they could steal from travelers. Before long the hermit blundered into them. The thieves were surprised, and even alarmed, at the sight of a man running, with nothing in pursuit. They came out of their ambush and stopped him, asking him what was the matter.

"I am fleeing, brothers," he said, "from the Devil, who is racing after me."

Now the bandits could not see anything following the devout old man, and they said, "Show us what is after you."

"I will," he said, and led them to the cave, at the same time begging them not to go near it. By this time, of course, the thieves were greatly interested, and insisted that they should be shown whatever it was that had caused such alarm.

"Here," he said, "is Death, which was running after me." And he pointed to the gold.

The villains were, of course, delighted. They naturally regarded the recluse as somewhat touched, and sent him on his way, while they reveled in their good fortune.

They then began to discuss what they should do with the booty, for they were afraid of leaving it alone again. Finally they decided that one of their number should take a little gold to the city and with it buy food and other necessities, and then they would proceed to the division of the spoils.

One of the ruffians volunteered to run the errand. He thought to himself, "When I am in town I can eat all I wish. Then I can poison the rest of the food, so that it kills the other two, and all the treasure will be mine."

While the rogue was away, however, his companions were also thinking. They decided that as soon as he returned, they would kill him and divide the spoils, so as to gain the additional third share that would otherwise be his.

The moment the first thief arrived back at the cave with the provisions, the two others fell upon him and stabbed him to death. Then they ate the food he had brought and died from the poison he had put into it.

So the gold, after all, did indeed spell death, as the hermit had predicted.

▪ *Themes* ▪

Money – Wealth – Greed – Betrayal – Death

▪ *For reflection and discussion* ▪

1. Why would the hermit use words such as 'devil' and 'death' in reference to the gold?

2. In what ways can the love of money be the source of all evil?

3. Read Proverbs 1:19. Do you think this statement is true?

_____

· *The Actor* ·

A famous actor was invited to a function where he was asked to recite for the pleasure of the guests. Having recited a few common verses, he asked if there was anything in particular they wanted to hear. After a moment or two, an old pastor asked to hear Psalm 23, "The Lord is my Shepherd". The actor paused for a moment and then said, "I will, but with one condition—that you will recite it also, after I have finished."

The pastor was taken by surprise. "I'm hardly a public speaker but, if you wish, I shall recite it too."

The actor began quite impressively. His voice was trained and his intonation was perfect. The audience was spellbound and when he finished, there was great applause from the guests. Now it was the old pastor's turn to recite the same psalm. His voice was not remarkable, his tone was not faultless, but when he finished, there was not a dry eye in the room.

The actor rose and his voice quavered as he said, "Ladies and gentlemen, I reached your eyes and your ears; he has reached your hearts. The difference is this: I know the Psalm but he knows the Shepherd."

· *Themes* ·

Communication—Mystical knowledge—Belief

· *For reflection and discussion* ·

1. What does the actor mean when he says, 'I know the Psalm, but he knows the Shepherd.'

2. Which is more important, to know about God, or to believe in God? Why?

3. Read Psalm 23. According to the Psalm, in what ways can God help us through life?

The Rival
· Shopkeepers ·

Once upon a time there were two shopkeepers who were bitter rivals. Their stores were across the street from each other, and they would spend each day sitting in the doorway, keeping an eye on each other's business. If one got a customer, he would smile in triumph at his rival.

One night, an angel appeared to one of the shopkeepers in a dream and said, "God has sent me to teach you a lesson. He will give you anything you ask for, but I want you to know that, whatever you get, your competitor across the street will get twice as much."

"Would you like to be wealthy?" said the angel. "You can be very wealthy, but he will be twice as rich. Do you want to lead a long and healthy life? You can, but his life will be longer and healthier. You can be famous, have children you will be proud of, whatever you desire. But whatever is granted to you, he will be granted twice as much."

The man frowned, thought for a moment, and said, "Alright, my request is this: strike me blind in one eye."

· Themes ·

Rivalry–Greed–Vindictiveness–Competition–Wealth

· For reflection and discussion ·

1. Do you think a person could gradually become so full of hatred that he or she would reach the extreme expressed in the story's last line?

2. If God were to grant you one wish, what would it be?

3. Read Luke 6:37–38. How does this exhortation relate to the story of the shopkeepers?

The Face at the Wall

──────── ∎ ──────── ∎ ────────

There was once a leper colony in the most heart-breaking and most hateful sense of the term. There were men with nothing to do, and for whom nothing could be done. They were lonely, abandoned men who could only prowl around their yard.

Yet one of these men kept a gleam in his eye. He could smile, and if you offered him something, could still say, "Thank you". There was this one single man, who was still a man, still human.

The Sister in charge was anxious to know the reason for this miracle. What kept him clinging to life? She watched him for a few days and she saw that there used to appear above the high, forbidding wall, every day, a face. A little tip of a woman's face, no bigger than a hand, but all smiles.

The man would be there, waiting to receive his smile, the food of his strength and support and his hope. He would smile back and then the head would disappear. Then his long wait for the next day would begin afresh.

When the Sister one day took them by surprise, he simply said, "She is my wife." And after a pause, he went on, "Before I came here, she hid me and looked after me with anything she could get. A native doctor had given her some paste to treat my disease. Every day she would smear my face with it — all except one tiny corner . . . just enough to put her lips to. But it couldn't last. They picked me up. She followed me here and when she comes to see me every day, I know that it is because of her that I can still go on living."

▪ *Themes* ▪

Relationships–Love–Support–Hope–Commitment–
Marriage–Suffering

▪ *For reflection and discussion* ▪

1. Do you believe it is possible that a loving relationship can sustain someone who is suffering?

2. Read I Corinthians 13:4–10. According to St. Paul, what are the characteristics of love?

My Butler's Mansion

Once there was a very rich man who dreamed he died and went to heaven. Saint Peter escorted him down a lovely street on which each house was magnificent. The rich man saw one house that was especially beautiful and asked who lived there. "That," said Saint Peter, "is the celestial home of your butler."

"Well," the man said smiling, "if my butler gets a place like that, I certainly look forward to seeing what my new home will be like."

Soon they came to a very small street where the houses were tiny and unpretentious. "You will live in that hut," said Saint Peter, pointing his finger.

"Me, live in that hovel!"

"This is the best we can do for you," explained the saint. "You must understand that we only build your home up here with the material you send ahead while you are still on earth."

▪ Themes ▪

Wealth—Justice—Greed—Lost opportunity—Readiness—
Life after death

▪ For reflection and discussion ▪

1. Why did the rich man expect to be given a magnificent home in heaven? What is this parable telling us about two very different value systems?

2. Give some examples of what you think is the 'material' you send ahead while you are still on earth.

3. Read Matthew 19:16–30. What does Jesus mean when he says: 'It is much harder for a rich person to enter the Kingdom of God than for a camel to go through the eye of a needle'?

— ▪ *The Rabbi's Gift* ▪ —

There was a famous monastery which had fallen on very hard times. Formerly its many buildings had been filled with young monks and its big church had resounded with the singing of the chant, but now it was deserted. People no longer came there to be nourished by prayer. A handful of old monks shuffled through the cloisters and praised their God with heavy hearts.

On the edge of the monastery woods, an old Rabbi had built a little hut. He would come there from time to time to fast and pray. No one ever spoke with him, but whenever he appeared, the word would be passed from monk to monk: "The Rabbi walks in the woods." And, for as long as he was there, the monks would feel sustained by his prayerful presence.

One day the Abbot decided to visit the Rabbi and to open his heart to him. So, after the morning Eucharist, he set out through the woods. As he approached the hut, the Abbot saw the Rabbi standing in the doorway, his arms outstretched in welcome. It was as though he had been waiting there for some time. The two embraced like long-lost brothers. Then they stepped back and just stood there, smiling at one another with smiles their faces could hardly contain.

After a while the Rabbi motioned the Abbot to enter. In the middle of the room was a wooden table with the Scriptures open on it. They sat there for a moment, in the presence of the Book. Then the Rabbi began to cry. The Abbot could not contain himself. He covered his face with his hands and began to cry, too. For the first time in his life, he cried his heart out. The two men sat there like lost children, filling the hut with their sobs and wetting the wood of the table with their tears.

After the tears had ceased to flow and all was quiet again, the Rabbi lifted his head. "You and your brothers are serving God with heavy hearts," he said. "You have come to ask a teaching of me. I will give you a teaching, but you can only repeat it once. After that, no one must ever say it aloud again."

The Rabbi looked straight at the Abbot and said, "The Messiah is among you."

For a while, all was silent. Then the Rabbi said, "Now you must go."

The Abbot left without a word and without ever looking back.

The next morning, the Abbot called his monks together in the chapter room. He told them he had received a teaching from the Rabbi who walks in the woods and that this teaching was never again to be spoken aloud. Then he looked at each of his brothers and said, "The Rabbi said that one of us is the Messiah."

The Monks were startled by this saying. "What could it mean?" they asked themselves. "Is Brother John the Messiah? Or Father Matthew? Or Brother Thomas? Am I the Messiah? What could this mean?"

They were all deeply puzzled by the Rabbi's teaching. But no one ever mentioned it again.

As time went by, the monks began to treat one another with very special reverence. There was a gentle, wholehearted, human quality about them now which was hard to describe but easy to notice. They lived with one another as men who had finally found something. But they prayed the Scriptures together as men who were always looking for something. Occasionally visitors found themselves deeply moved by the life of these monks.

Before long, people were coming from far and wide to be nourished by the prayer life of the monks and young men were asking, once again, to become part of the community.

By then, the Rabbi no longer walked in the woods. His hut had fallen into ruins. But, somehow or other, the old monks who had taken his teaching to heart still felt sustained by his prayerful presence.

▪ *Themes* ▪

Communication–Ecumenism–Community–Spirituality–Prayer

▪ *For reflection and discussion* ▪

1. What do you think the Rabbi meant when he said: 'The Messiah is among you'?

2. Did you expect the monks' attitudes towards each other to change?

3. Think of a group of which you are a member—your family, church group, class, or other. What would you imagine your group's reaction would be to the message, 'The Lord is among you'?

—— • *The Window* • ——

Two men, both seriously ill, were in the same small ward of a great hospital. It was quite a small ward, with just room for the pair of them . . . a door opening on the corridor, and one window looking out on the world.

Now, one of the men was allowed to sit up for an hour in the morning and an hour in the afternoon, and his bed was next to the window. But the other man had to spend all his time flat on his back. And both of them had to be kept quiet and still. Of course, one of the disadvantages of their condition was that they were not allowed to do much: no reading, no radio, no television . . . they just had to keep quiet and still . . . just the two of them. Well, they used to talk for hours and hours . . . about their wives and children, their homes, their jobs, what they did during the war, where they'd been on holidays . . . all that sort of thing. And every morning and afternoon when the man in the bed next to the window was propped up for his hour, he would describe what he could see outside. And the other man almost began to live for these hours.

The window apparently overlooked a park, with a lake, and there were the usual ducks and swans, children throwing them bread and sailing model yachts, young lovers walking hand in hand beneath the trees. And there were flowers, mainly roses, but with a magnificent border of dahlias and marigolds—bronze and gold and crimson. In the far corner was a tennis court, and at times the games were really good. And there was cricket, not quite up to Test Match standard, but better than nothing. And there was a bowling green, and right at the back, a row of shops with a view of the city behind.

And the man on his back would listen to all of this, enjoying every minute . . . how a child nearly fell into the lake, how beautiful the girls were in their summer dresses, and then an exciting tennis match. And he got so that he could almost see what was happening out there.

Then one afternoon, when a batsman was knocking some slow bowling all over the cricket ground, the thought struck him: Why should the man next to the window have all the pleasure of seeing what was going on? Why shouldn't he get the chance? He felt ashamed, and tried not to think like that but the more he tried the worse it became . . . Until, in a few days, it all turned sour: why wasn't *he* near the window?

And he brooded by day, and stayed awake by night and grew even more seriously ill, with none of the doctors understanding why.

Then, one night, as he stared at the ceiling, the other man suddenly woke up, coughing and choking, the fluid congesting in his lungs, his hands groping for the button that would bring the night nurse running.

But the man watched without moving. What had he ever done to deserve to have the bed by the window? The coughing racked the darkness . . . on and on . . . choking off . . . then stopped . . . the sound of breathing stopped. And the other man continued to stare at the ceiling.

In the morning, the nurses came with water for their wash . . . they found the other man dead, and took away his body, quietly, with no fuss.

As soon as it seemed decent, the man asked could he be moved to the bed next to the window. And they moved him, tucked him in, and made him quite comfortable . . . and left him alone to be quiet and still.

The minute they'd gone, he levered himself up on one elbow, painfully and laboriously, gasping . . . and looked out the window.

It faced a blank wall.

▪ *Themes* ▪

Envy–Relationships–Imagination–Positive and negative thinking

▪ *For reflection and discussion* ▪

1. Why do you think the man kept making believe that he could see all the beautiful scenes from his window?

2. How would the other patient have felt when he realized the window faced a blank wall? Try to name the emotions he must have experienced. Would some of those emotions have stayed with him even if the view had been as beautiful as described?

3. Could it be said that *two* deaths take place in this story? . . . Read Psalm 116, and reflect on your feelings about trusting God in times of serious illness and suffering.

A True
Confession

Several ministers from a small town were out fishing in a boat. As the fish weren't biting, they fell to talking. Since they had counseled their parishioners for many years that confession is good for the soul, they decided they would practise what they had been preaching. Each decided to confess his secret sin to the others.

The first said that his great fault was language; he still had trouble once in a while holding back improper words. The second minister admitted that his weakness was materialism; he was too fond of money and it was his first and main consideration in changing parishes. The third preacher broke the news of an addiction to petty gambling on anything from golf to football.

The last minister, who was the helmsman on the small craft, had by this time turned the boat toward shore and had increased the speed. One of the confessors said, "What's the hurry? Besides, you haven't made your confession." The minister replied, "Well, you see, my sin is gossip, and I just can't wait to get home!"

▪ Themes ▪

Gossip – Secrecy – Sin – Humility – Addiction

▪ For reflection and discussion ▪

1. Is there truth in this statement: 'A sharp tongue is the only tool that grows sharper with constant use'?

2. Read James 3:3–10. What is your reaction to the way the writer describes the 'tongue'.

3. Which people in society are most apt to be hurt by gossip? What can each of us do about it?

_____

▪ *One Wish* ▪

Once upon a time, on an island kingdom, there lived a very old man. His eyes showed the wisdom of the years and though he was ragged in appearance, there was a gentleness about him.

One day as he was walking through the forest, he was attacked by a band of robbers. They beat him, took the little money he had, and left him to die by the roadside.

The old man remained by the edge of the road, bruised and sore, for quite some hours until three soldiers happened to come past. They helped the old man to his feet, attended to his bruises and escorted him home.

A few days later, the soldiers returned to see how the old man was faring. He had nearly recovered and was so grateful to them that he said, "I owe my life to you gentlemen. In return I will grant you whatever you wish. But be very cautious," he continued, "I will grant you only one wish each."

The soldiers thought the old man was perhaps *too* old. Who could grant another's wish? But they had nothing to lose, so they humored him.

The first soldier, who was rather poor, said, "Old man, I have thought carefully and I wish for wealth." As soon as he had made his wish, a trunk full of treasure appeared beside him. The wish had come true! They were all astounded. The soldier thanked the old man sincerely and went home with his riches.

As he left, the old man closed his eyes and he could see that the soldier would live comfortably with his wealth. He would have many friends and the best food and wine. But the old man could also see that the soldier's riches would eventually run out and he would lose his friends. He would be poor again!

Now the second soldier, who was rather ugly, went to the old man and said, "Old man, I have thought carefully too and my wish is to be handsome." As soon as he had made his wish, the soldier felt his face change—he had become remarkably handsome! He thanked the old man sincerely and went home with his good looks.

As he left, the old man closed his eyes and he could see that the soldier would live happily with his good looks. He would have many friends and would be very popular with women. But the old man could also see that as the soldier grew older, he would lose his good looks and his friends. He would be ugly again!

Now the third soldier was rather poor *and* ugly. He also wished his wish, thanked the old man sincerely and went home. As he left, the old man closed his eyes and he could see that this soldier would remain rather poor and ugly all his life. But he would live in peace, for this wish was simply to be happy with whatever he had.

▪ *Themes* ▪

Happiness–Wisdom–Wealth–Poverty–Contentment–
Good looks

▪ *For reflection and discussion* ▪

1. What signs of wishful thinking and get-rich-quick schemes do you notice in our world today? Do most people believe that money would make them really happy?

2. If you were granted one wish, what would it be? How long would its effects last?

3. Read Proverbs 3:13–18. Why do you think this reading suggests that 'wisdom' will make a person happy?

———————————

▪ *The Picture* ▪

There was once a boy who wanted to say things, but no one understood. He often wanted to explain things, but no one had time to listen. So he drew. Sometimes he would just draw and it wasn't anything. He wanted to carve it in stone or write it in the sky. He would be out on the grass and look up in the sky and it would be only him and the sky and the things inside that needed saying.

One day he drew *the* picture. It was beautiful. He kept it under his pillow and would let no one see it. He would look at it every night and think about it, and when it was dark, and his eyes were closed, he could still see it. It was all of him and he loved it.

When he started school he brought it with him; not to show anyone, but just to have it with him like a friend. He sat in a square, brown desk like all the other square, brown desks and he thought it should be red. His classroom was a square, brown room. Like all the other rooms. And it was tight and closed and stiff.

The boy hated to hold the pencil and the chalk, with his arm stiff and his feet flat on the floor, stiff, with the teacher watching. Then he had to write numbers which weren't anything. They were worse than the letters that could be something if you put them together. The numbers were tight and square and he hated the whole thing.

The teacher came and spoke to him. She told him to wear a tie like all the other boys. He said he didn't like the ties and she said that didn't matter. After that the class drew. The boy drew all yellow and it was the way he felt about morning. And it was beautiful. The teacher came and smiled at him. "What's this?" she said. "Why don't you draw something like Ken's drawing?

89

Isn't that beautiful?"

It was all questions.

After that his mother bought him a tie and he always drew aeroplanes and rocket ships like everyone else. He threw the old picture away. And when he lay out alone looking at the sky, it was big and blue and all of everything, but *he* wasn't anymore.

He was square inside and brown, and his hands were stiff, and he was like everyone else. The thing inside him that needed saying didn't need saying anymore. It had stopped pushing. It was crushed. Stiff. Like everything else.

▪ *Themes* ▪

Creativity–Conformity–Personal growth and development–
Education–Individuality–Social pressure

▪ *For reflection and discussion* ▪

1. What pressures make it difficult for individuals to paint their own pictures in life?

2. Is it possible to express one's individuality without rejecting the values of the school, home or society?

3. Give some examples of Jesus accepting the 'individual'.

The Miller, his Son and their Donkey

A miller and his son were travelling with their donkey to the market to sell him. They had not gone far when they met some women coming from the town, talking as they walked.

"Isn't that strange!" said one of the women, when they drew near. "Have you ever seen such silly people? Walking along the hard road when they could be riding on the back of the donkey!" The miller heard what they were saying and quietly told his son to get up on the donkey's back and they continued on their way.

Soon they passed a group of elderly men sitting by the roadside. "You see what I mean," said one of them as the miller and his son passed by. "The young generation has no respect for old people these days. When I was young, you would never dare ride while your father had to walk." The miller quietly asked his son to get off the donkey and he took his place.

They had not gone very far when they met a husband and wife. "Look at that mean old man," they both cried out. "How can you ride while your son has to walk? The poor little boy can hardly keep up with you." The miller quietly lifted the son onto the donkey and together they rode towards the market.

As they reached the market they met a shopkeeper who said, "Tell me, is that your donkey?"

"Yes," replied the miller.

"Why do you treat him so harshly? Two healthy people like you could carry him more easily than he can carry you!"

The miller and his son got down from the donkey's back and firstly tied his legs together, then they slipped a pole through the rope and heaved the donkey onto their shoulders.

They had not walked much further before they came to a

bridge which led to the market. The bridge was crowded with people and they all began laughing at the sight of the miller and his son carrying the donkey between them. The noise frightened the poor donkey and he kicked himself free of the ropes that tied his feet together but fell over the wall of the bridge into the river below.

There was nothing the miller and his son could do but go home again. "Next time," muttered the miller, "I'll do as I please."

▪ *Themes* ▪

Peer pressure – Self-assertiveness – Independent thinking

▪ *For reflection and discussion* ▪

1. What was the miller's problem?

2. To what extent should one listen to the advice of others?

3. In what circumstances can the advice of others lead to difficulties?

— • *A Jar of Wine* • —

This is the story of a parish priest who was well liked and admired by everyone in his village. One day he received a letter from the bishop stating that he was to be transferred to another town.

The villagers were sorry to hear this news because he was a good and kindly man. They called a meeting of the village council to decide what gift they would offer him on his departure. There were many suggestions, but the most favorable one was to give the priest some wine.

A huge earthen jar was placed in the town square and each villager was invited to pour into the jar a bottle of his best wine. What a fine gift this would be for a lover of wine, as the priest was reputed to be!

So the jar was left in the square for a few days and the villagers came and poured in their bottles of wine.

One villager, however, thought to himself, "If I pour into the jar a bottle of water, it will be mixed with the fine wine and no one will know the difference." And so he did.

On the last day the good people gathered around in the square to present the gift to the priest and bid him a fond farewell. He thanked them for their loyalty and their generosity and then poured himself a glass of what was to be the finest wine he had ever tasted. But all that passed his lips was pure water!

• *Themes* •

Responsibility–Generosity–Honesty

▪ *For reflection and discussion* ▪

1. What would have happened if the priest had exclaimed, 'Why this is just plain water!'? What effects do you think this 'moment of truth' would have had on the townspeople?

2. What would society be like if none of us took responsibility for 'pulling our own weight'?

3. Explain this old English proverb: 'The hand that gives, gathers.'

The Contest
for Youth

There is a West Indian folk tale about a contest for youth. The young men of the village were sent off to search for the most beautiful thing in the world, and to return to show it to the elders.

One young enthusiast named Amarli Bakoff raced for the distant hills which had always fascinated him. He climbed higher and higher, up through the forest and across the scrubland until he came to snowfields for the first time in his life. "Surely," he thought, as he reached the dazzling whiteness, "this must be the most beautiful thing in the world!" He plunged his hand into the stinging coldness and clutched a handful of snow in its marvelous purity.

With his hand held tightly closed, he raced back to the village, eager to be on time for the judging of the contest. The villagers were assembled, and the elders were inspecting the priceless treasures which the other youths had discovered: jewels, silks, marvels of art and craft, and wonders of nature. Suddenly Amarli Bakoff broke into their midst.

"What have you brought us?" they asked excitedly.

"See!" he cried triumphantly—and he opened his hand.

There was nothing there. They saw nothing. Only Amarli Bakoff knew the meaning of what had happened.

"The most beautiful thing in the world," he said, "is what hand cannot hold."

▪ *Themes* ▪

Values—Wealth—Achievement—Beauty

▪ *For reflection and discussion* ▪

1. Do you agree that 'the most beautiful thing in the world is what the hand cannot hold'. Why? Why not?

2. If you were Amarli Bakoff, what would you have brought back?

───────────────

— ▪ *The Greedy Boy* ▪ —

There was once a young boy who was asked to do a job for a neighbor. When he finished, she said to him, "Go to the kitchen and you will find a jar full of nuts and figs. Take some for yourself. You have been a great help to me."

The boy went into the kitchen, found the jar and put his hand in to help himself to as many as he could hold. When he tried to take his hand out of the jar, however, he found that the opening was too narrow for his fistful of sweets to pass through.

"What will I do?" he cried.

At this point the woman came into the kitchen and saw the predicament the boy was in. "There's nothing to cry about," she said. "Just let go of a few of them, and then you'll be able to draw out the rest."

▪ *Themes* ▪

Greed–Moderation–Wisdom

▪ *For reflection and discussion* ▪

1. Explain the 'predicament' the boy was in. Can you think of more complex but similar-type situations?

2. Do you think it is true that if you try to take too much from life, you may end up with nothing?

The Hiding
of Divinity

According to an old Hindu legend, there was a time when all human beings were gods, but they so abused their divinity that Brahma, the chief god, decided to take it away from them and hide it where they would never find it. Where to hide it became the big question.

When the lesser gods were called in council to consider this question, they said, "We will bury human divinity deep in the earth."

But Brahma said, "No, that will not do, for there will be people who will dig deep down into the earth and find it."

Then they said, "Well, we will sink human divinity into the deepest ocean."

But again Brahma replied, "No, not there, for people will learn to dive into the deepest waters, will search out the ocean bed, and will find it."

Then the lesser gods said, "We will take it to the top of the highest mountain and there hide it."

Again Brahma replied, "No, for people will eventually climb every high mountain on earth. They will be sure to find it and take it up again for themselves."

Then the lesser gods gave up and concluded, "We do not know where to hide it, for it seems there is no place on earth or in the sea that human beings will not eventually reach."

But Brahma said, "Here is what we will do with human divinity. We will hide it deep down in every person, for no one will think to look for it there." Ever since then, the legend concludes, men and women have been going up and down the earth, climbing, digging, diving, exploring, searching for something that is already in themselves.

Two thousand years ago, a man named Jesus found it and shared its secret—but in the movement that sprang up in his name, the divine presence in us has been the best kept secret of the ages.

▪ *Themes* ▪

Inner worth—Self-esteem

▪ *For reflection and discussion* ▪

1. How would you explain the meaning of the word 'divinity'?

2. What do you understand by the statement: 'divinity is hidden within the human person'?

3. In Genesis I:26, the writer says that we are created in the image of God. In your own life experience have there been times when human behavior seemed to affirm this fact? Times when people's actions seemed, on the contrary, quite 'ungodly'?

The Two • *Brothers* •

Two brothers worked together on a family farm. One was unmarried and the other married with children. They shared what they grew equally as they always did—produce and profit. But one day the single brother said to himself, "You know, it's not right that we should share the produce equally, and the profit too. After all, I'm all alone, just by myself and my needs are simple. But there is my poor brother with a wife and all those children."

So in the middle of the night he took a sack of grain from his bin, crept over the field between their houses and dumped it into his brother's bin.

Meanwhile, unknown to him, his brother had the same thought. He said to himself, "It is not right that we should share produce and profit equally. After all, I am married and I have my wife to look after me and my children for years to come. But my brother has no one, and no one to take care of his future."

So he too, in the middle of the night, began taking a sack of grain from his bin and sneaking across the field to deposit it in his brother's.

And both were puzzled for years as to why their supply did not dwindle. Well, one night it just so happened that they both set out for each other's house at the same time. In the dark they bumped into each other carrying their sacks. Each was startled, but then it slowly dawned on them what was happening. They dropped their sacks and embraced one another.

Suddenly the dark sky lit up and a voice from heaven spoke, "Here at last is the place where I will build my Temple. For where brothers meet in love, there my Presence shall dwell."

▪ *Themes* ▪

Love–Generosity–Relationships–Presence of God

▪ *For reflection and discussion* ▪

1. What feelings does this story leave you with?

2. Read Matthew 6:2–4. In what way does the writer of Matthew's Gospel suggest that Christians should give?

In the
Wrong File

About fifteen years ago, [relates Fr. John Powell, SJ,] I stood watching my university students file into the classroom for our first session in the Theology of Faith. That was the day I first saw Tommy. My eyes and my mind both blinked. He was combing his long flaxen hair, which hung *six inches* below his shoulders. It was the first time I had ever seen a boy with hair that long. I guess it was just coming into fashion then. I know in my mind that it isn't what's on your head but in it that counts, but on that day I was unprepared and my emotions flipped. I immediately filed Tommy under S for strange . . . very strange.

Tommy turned out to be the atheist in residence in my Theology of Faith course. He constantly objected to, smirked at, or whined about the possibility of an unconditionally loving Father-God. We lived with each other in relative peace for one semester, although I admit he was for me at times a serious pain in the back pew. When he came up at the end of the course to turn in his final exam, he asked in a slightly cynical tone: "Do you think I'll ever find God?"

I decided instantly on a little shock therapy. "No!" I said very emphatically.

"Oh," he responded, "I thought that was the product you were pushing."

I let him get five steps from the classroom door and then called out: "Tommy! I don't think you'll ever find Him, but I am absolutely certain that He will find you!"

He shrugged a little and left my class and my life (temporarily). I felt slightly disappointed at the thought that he had missed my clever line: "He will find you!" At least I thought it was clever.

Later I heard that Tom was graduated and I was duly grateful. Then a sad report. I heard that Tommy had terminal cancer. Before I could search him out, he came to see me. His body was badly wasted, and the long hair had all fallen out as a result of chemotherapy. But his eyes were bright and his voice was firm, for the first time, I think. "Tommy, I've thought about you so often. I hear you are sick!" I blurted out.

"Oh, yes, very sick. I have cancer in both lungs. It's a matter of weeks."

"Can you talk about it, Tom?"

"Sure, what would you like to know?"

"What's it like to be only twenty-four and dying?"

"Well, it could be worse."

"Like what?"

"Well, like being fifty and having no values or ideals, like being fifty and thinking that booze, seducing women, and making money are the real 'biggies' in life."

I began to look through my mental file cabinet under S where I had filed Tom as strange. (I swear that everybody I try to reject by classification God sends back into my life to educate me.)

"But what I really came to see you about," Tom said, "is something you said to me on the last day of class." (He remembered!)

He continued, "I asked you if you thought I would ever find God and you said, 'No!' which surprised me. Then you said, 'But He will find you.' I thought about that a lot, even though my search for God was hardly intense at that time. (My 'clever' line. He thought about that a lot!)

"But when the doctors removed a lump from my groin and told me that it was malignant, then I got serious about locating God. And when the malignancy spread into my vital organs, I really began banging bloody fists against the bronze doors of heaven. But God did not come out. In fact, nothing happened. Did you ever try anything for a long time with great effort and with no success? You get psychologically glutted, fed up with trying. And then you quit. Well, one day I woke up, and instead of throwing a few more futile appeals over that high brick wall to a God who may be or may not be there, I just quit. I decided that I didn't really care . . . about God, about an afterlife, or anything like that.

"I decided to spend what time I had left doing something

more profitable. I thought about you and your class and I remembered something else you had said: 'The essential sadness is to go through life without loving. But it would be almost equally sad to go through life and leave this world without ever telling those you loved that you had loved them.'

"So I began with the hardest one: my dad. He was reading a newspaper when I approached him.

"Dad . . ."

"Yes, what?" he asked without lowering the newspaper.

"Dad, I would like to talk with you."

"Well, talk."

"I mean . . . It's really important."

The newspaper came down three slow inches. "What is it?"

"Dad, I love you. I just wanted you to know that."

Tom smiled at me and said with obvious satisfaction, as though he felt a warm and secret joy flowing inside of him: "The newspaper fluttered to the floor. Then my father did two things I could never remember him ever doing before. He cried and he hugged me. And we talked all night, even though he had to go to work the next morning. It felt so good to be close to my father, to see his tears, to feel his hug, to hear him say that he loved me.

"It was easier with my mother and little brother. They cried with me, too, and we hugged each other, and started saying real nice things to each other. We shared the things we had been keeping secret for so many years. I was only sorry about one thing: that I had waited so long. Here I was, in the shadow of death, and I was just beginning to open up to all the people I had actually been close to.

"Then, one day I turned around and God was there. He didn't come to me when I pleaded with him. I guess I was like an animal trainer holding out a hoop, 'C'mon, jump through. C'mon, I'll give you three days . . . three weeks.' Apparently God does things in his own way and at his own hour.

"But the important thing is that He was there. He found me. You were right. He found me even after I stopped looking for Him."

"Tommy," I practically gasped, "I think you are saying something very important and much more universal than you realize. To me, at least, you are saying that the surest way to find God is not to make him a private possession, a problem solver, or an instant consolation in time of need, but rather by opening to love. You know, Saint John said that. He said 'God is love, and anyone who lives in love is living with God and God is living in him.'

"Tom, could I ask you a favor? You know, when I had you in class you were a real pain. But (laughingly) you can make it all up to me now. Would you come into my present Theology of Faith course and tell them what you have just told me? If I told them the same thing, it wouldn't be half as effective as if you were to tell them."

"Oooh . . . I was ready for you, but I don't know if I'm ready for your class."

"Tom, think about it. If and when you are ready, give me a call."

In a few days Tommy called, said he was ready for the class, that he wanted to do that for God and for me. So we scheduled a date. However, he never made it. . . .

• Themes •

Relationships–Finding God–Values–Faith–Love–Dying

• For reflection and discussion •

1. Has experience shown you that people often get put in the 'wrong file' by parents, teachers, neighbors, employers, etc.? If you can think of any one instance, try to recall what it was that brought about a reversal of opinion.

2. To what extent do you believe this statement is true: 'The essential sadness is to go through life without loving'?

3. Why do you think many people find it hard to express love to those closest to them?

▪ *The Bat* ▪

Once there was a war between beasts and birds. Bat was on the birds' side. In the first battle, the birds were badly beaten. As soon as Bat saw that the battle was going against them, he crept away, hid under a log, and stayed there 'till the fight was over.

When the animals were going home, Bat slipped in among them.

After they had gone some distance, they noticed him and asked one another, "How is this? Bat is one of those who fought against us."

Bat heard them, and he said, "Oh, no! I am one of you; I don't belong to the bird people. Did you ever see one of those people who had double teeth? Go and look in their mouths and see if they have. If you find one bird with double teeth, you can say that I belong to the bird people. But I don't; I am one of you."

The beasts didn't say anything more; they let Bat stay with them.

Soon after, there was another battle; in that battle the birds won. As Bat's side was getting beaten, he slipped away and hid under a log. When the battle was over and the birds were going home, Bat went in among them.

When they noticed him, they said, "You are our enemy; we saw you fighting against us."

"Oh no," said Bat, "I am one of you; I don't belong to those beasts. Did you ever see one of those people who had wings?"

The birds didn't say anything more; they let him stay with them.

So Bat went back and forth as long as the war lasted.

At the end of the war, the birds and beasts held a council to see what to do with Bat. At last they said to him, "Hereafter,

106

you will fly around alone at night, and will never have any friends, among neither those that fly nor those that walk!''

■ *Themes* ■

Loyalty–Friendship–Cowardice–Opportunists–Relationships

■ *For reflection and discussion* ■

1. How important is loyalty in relationships?

2. Today Bat would probably be labeled an extreme *opportunist*! In what areas of modern life might he show up?

3. Read John 15:12–17. What does the passage say about Jesus' view of friendship?

───── • *Born Blind* • ─────

Darkness. You have not felt it as I have, completely, blackly, without the tiniest glimmer or wink of light. For I was born blind.

My earliest memory is of hands. I did not know hands as you do, colored, textured, moving with life. For me, hands were mysterious, solid extensions of the blackness. Hands were hard, patting or prying parts of the blackness which reached out and touched me. Everything was darkness. Flowers were soft and scented flutterings of darkness; walls were where the darkness hardened and would not let me pass; nails and knives were bits of blackness leaping out to cut me if I were not careful; stones were the hiding lumps that sought to trip my feet and tumble me to the wide, flat hardness that other men called earth.

Happily, I was not alone. As a child my parents cared for and protected me from the dangers of my darkness. As I grew older I had friends, not many, but some, who would call on me and tell me of the life I could not see. They even described my own face to me for I did not really know myself.

It was my friends who told me the news of Jesus of Nazareth as he traveled the countryside. And it was with some of them that I went to Jesus when he came to Bethsaida.

The din of the crowd was deafening, and shoulders buffeted me like waves as my friends strained to see the Prophet. I moved with them, trying to draw close enough to hear his words. There were so many people that I could follow his progress by their voices as they rose with his approach. Everyone was clamoring, straining to reach him, and it seemed that I could not hope to get close enough to hear. All was confusion. I do not think half the people knew why they had come. My friends had told me they did not know. The Prophet merely attracted them, they said. He might be a great man, even sent by God, but of course one could not be certain. Yet, if you believed some of the stories, the things people said that he could do . . .

Suddenly the idea struck me. I gripped a friend's arm and whispered my decision almost before I realized it.

"Take me to him."

"What?"

"Take me to the Prophet. If it is true, then he can help me."

"What are you saying?" another beside me asked. "Help you how?"

And then I knew; I knew what I wanted more than anything else. I wanted it so badly that I would be willing to die a moment after receiving it. "He can make me see," I said and felt my breathlessness at the very thought of it. "Please, if you are my friends," I said and gripped their arms tightly.

Jesus was coming closer, and it was more difficult to move as we struggled toward the edge of the crowd.

"We are at the road," a friend finally said, and I felt its hard surface where the grass ended.

Despite the greater number of people, it was not as loud here as it had been on the outskirts of the crowd. I was trying to fathom the strange quiet when I heard my friend's voice beside me. He was answering a question I had not heard. ". . . to touch him, Master," he said. "Will you place your hands on our friend?"

They were asking, and my heart stopped in my throat. They were asking him for me. The silence was complete. Why was it so quiet? What was happening? Instinctively, I put my hands out before me.

A hand locked about my own and I stopped. I had never felt a grip like this. It was steady, strong, but not the strong, hard darkness I had felt before. This hand was different. It came through the darkness from a great power beyond. It was not part of the darkness; it passed through the darkness as if it were not there.

Suddenly I became more frightened than I had ever been, frightened that I would lose that hand. I seized it with my other and held firmly as it pulled me forward.

The sounds of the people faded, and I wanted to put my hands to the sides of my head because I was becoming dizzy. But I dared not let go. I could not tell whether I was walking, but as long as I held on I knew that I would be safe. I would hold on forever.

Yet when the hand slipped from mine, mine somehow relaxed. It is all right, something told me. He is not leaving.

There were sounds. He was picking up dirt, that hard blackness upon which I walked every day. What worth did that have?

He was moistening the dirt, my friends said. Next minute I felt the mud on my eyes, cool, thick, and mysterious. Then his hands pressed peacefully upon my shoulders, and I heard his voice close to my face.

"Can you see anything?"

Strange. The darkness was falling into forms and behind and between the forms . . . that must be light. The forms moved, back and forth through the haze, filmy forms, tall like trees which I had felt and tried to climb as a boy. They were people, people moving.

I tried to tell him, to describe what it was, but how could I take it from my mind to show him? The hands touched my eyes again, covered them peacefully, and as they parted, colors burst about me.

People! Faces! Blue . . . the sky! Green everywhere! The colors . . . burning, glistening, pulsing, jumping, flashing everywhere! So that is what people look like, what my body looks like, what *he* looks like! I raised my gaze up the dusty cloak and into that face. His eyes were watching me. His eyes like my own. Like my eyes . . .

Oh God! Everything blurred and a warmness filled my face, but I was not frightened. It was good. They were tears, tears from my eyes that could see. I raised my hand to touch them. No, I would let them flow. It was good to cry from sheer happiness. I heard the people shouting excitedly. Their cries were everywhere.

". . . sees!" they said. "He sees! He can see! He can see!"

"I can see," I whispered. "I can see everything." And as I continued to gaze into the eyes of Jesus, I suddenly realized I had been given the gift of *two* kinds of vision that day.

▪ *Themes* ▪

Faith – Disability – Miracles – Healing

▪ *For reflection and discussion* ▪

1. The story you have just read takes you inside the blind man. Does this sharing of his thoughts and feelings enrich your reading of the parallel Gospel stories: John 9:1–41, Mark 8:22–26, 10:46–52, Luke 18:35–43?

2. To what extent is it true to say that we are all disabled to a certain degree?

3. What were the 'two' kinds of vision the blind person received?

The Cat in ▪ *the Lifeboat* ▪

A cat named William got a job as copy cat on a daily paper and was surprised to learn that every other cat on the paper was named Tom, Dick, or Harry. He soon found out that he was the only cat named William in town. The fact of his singularity went to his head, and he began confusing it with distinction.

It got so that whenever he saw or heard the name William, he thought it referred to him. His fantasies grew wilder and wilder, and he came to believe that he was the Will of Last Will and Testament, and the Willy of Willy Nilly, and the cat who put the cat in catnip. He finally became convinced that Cadillacs were Catillacs because of him.

William became so lost in his daydreams that he no longer heard the editor of the paper when he shouted, "Copy cat!" and he became not only a ne'er-do-well, but a ne'er-do-anything. "You're fired," the editor told him one morning when he showed up for dreams.

"God will provide," said William jauntily.

"God has his eye on the sparrow," said the editor.

"So've I," said William smugly.

William went to live with a cat-crazy woman who had nineteen other cats, but they could not stand William's egotism or the tall tales of his mythical exploits, honors, blue ribbons, silver cups, and medals, and so they all left the woman's house and went to live happily in huts and hovels. The cat-crazy woman changed her will and made William her sole heir, which seemed only natural to him, since he believed that all wills were drawn in his favor. "I am eight feet tall," William told her one day, and she smiled and said, "I should say you are, and I am going to take you on a trip around the world and show you off to everybody."

William and his mistress sailed one bitter March day on the S.S. *Forlorna*, which ran into heavy weather, high seas, and a hurricane. At midnight the cargo shifted in the towering seas, the ship listed menacingly, SOS calls were frantically sent out, rockets were fired into the sky, and the officers began running up and down companionways and corridors shouting, "Abandon ship!" And then another shout arose, which seemed only natural to the egotistical cat. It was, his vain ears told him, the loud repetition of "William and Children first!"

Since William figured no lifeboat would be launched until he was safe and sound, he dressed leisurely, putting on white tie and tails, and then sauntered out on deck. He leaped lightly into a lifeboat that was being lowered, and found himself in the company of a little boy named Johnny Green and another little boy named Tommy Trout, and their mothers, and other children and their mothers. "Toss that cat overboard!" cried the sailor in charge of the lifeboat, and Johnny Green threw him overboard, but Tommy Trout pulled him back in.

"Let me have that tomcat," said the sailor, and he took William in his big right hand and threw him, like a long incompleted forward pass, about forty yards from the tossing lifeboat.

When William came to in the icy water, he had gone down for the twenty-fourth time, and had thus lost eight of his lives, so he only had one left. With his remaining life and strength he swam and swam until at last he reached the sullen shore of a somber island inhabited by surly tigers, lions, and other great cats. As William lay drenched and panting on the shore, a jaguar and a lion walked up to him and asked him who he was and where he came from. Alas, William's dreadful experience in the lifeboat and the sea had produced traumatic amnesia, and he could not remember who he was or where he came from.

"We'll call him Nobody," said the jaguar.

"Nobody from Nowhere," said the lion.

And so William lived among the great cats on the island until he lost his ninth life in a bar-room brawl with a young panther who had asked him what his name was and where he came from and got what he considered an uncivil answer.

The great cats buried William in an unmarked grave because, as the jaguar said, "What's the good of putting up a stone reading, 'Here lies Nobody from Nowhere'?"

▪ *Themes* ▪

Self-importance – Over-confidence – Imagination – Egotism

▪ *For reflection and discussion* ▪

1. What is the moral of this fable?

2. Notice the role that daydreams and fantasies played in the growth of William's inflated self-image. Do you feel that daydreaming can be a dangerous habit?

3. Read I Peter 5:5–7. From your own experience is there a connection between humility and concern for others?

The Sermon
of the Mouse

The day had finally arrived. Everyone in the congregation was waiting expectantly. The negotiations had taken months, but finally everything had been worked out. It wasn't every congregation in the country that could have an opportunity like this. It was a rare visit from a very well-known celebrity.

The pastor and his guest mounted the platform. The first hymn was sung. Then the pastor rose. "I'm sure everyone is aware who our guest speaker is this morning," he said.

Aware? How could anyone help being aware? There were posters all over town. There was a big yellow and black banner stretched across the entry to the parking lot. Seating in the sanctuary had been assigned on a reservation basis with preferential treatment given to members in good standing. An overflow crowd was watching the service on closed-circuit television. Everybody knew about it.

"It isn't often," said the pastor, "that we have an opportunity to meet someone who has become a legend in his own time. Starting back in the bleak years of the depression, with a shoestring budget and a very simple plan, our guest, with hard work and contagious enthusiasm, built an empire for himself that rivals that of Howard Hughes. His name is a household word; he is admired by young and old alike; and he has even survived his mentor. He reigns over a multimillion dollar business venture that was so successful in southern California that he established an even more spectacular venture in Florida. By now, I'm sure you know whom I am talking about. We are so honored to have Mickey Mouse with us today to share with us the secrets of Disneyland's success. We hope that our church will be stimulated and helped by his story."

A hush came over the congregation as this famous mouse rose to his feet, cleared his throat, and began his sermon.

"Thank you for inviting me to come to your church. I must admit at first I was surprised that a church would ask me to give a sermon. Oh, I have been invited to religion-class contests where they give each new person a Mickey Mouse hat and expect me to shake hands with everyone and act funny, but a sermon is something new.

"But after I thought it out, I realized that maybe Disneyland and the church did have a lot in common. As I began to organize my thoughts, I saw how ingenious it was to invite me to share. I really believe that if your church were to apply our principles you could become as successful as Disneyland.

"First, make sure your enterprise seems exciting, even dangerous; but be quick to let your people know that there really is no danger involved. Give the illusion of great risk, but make sure everything is perfectly safe.

"Second, admit that you are in the entertainment business. People won't care what you say as long as they're entertained. Keep your people happy. Don't tell them anything negative. And don't make demands on them. Just keep them diverted from the ugly reality of today's world, and they will keep coming back for more.

"Third, make everything look religious. Make the religious experience so elaborate, so intricate, so complex that only the professionals can pull it off; and all the laymen can do is stand around with their mouths open and watch. People would rather watch an imitation mechanical bird sing than a real bird, anyway. They would rather watch worship than do it.

"Fourth and finally, pretend that there are no problems. At Disneyland we dress up our security guards as smiling rabbits or friendly bears because we don't want anyone's experience at Disneyland to be ruined by the sight of law enforcement personnel. Disguise your problems and failures behind a warm smile and a firm handshake. Leave them at home, and let the chuch be a happy place where there aren't any ugly problems.

"People today want good, clean entertainment. They want an environment that is safe for children, and they want a place that is safe for their family and friends. I am so glad to see that the church is moving in this direction. Thank you, and God bless you."

▪ *Themes* ▪
Religion–Church–Values–Worship–Pretence

▪ *For reflection and discussion* ▪

1. Do you see any parallel between the Church and Disneyland?

2. Do Christians expect to be 'entertained' when they go to church?

3. Would you rather 'watch' worship than do it?

4. What risks are there in being a Christian today?

The Richest
Man in the
Valley

There was a wealthy lord who lived in the Scottish Highlands. He was more than richly endowed with this world's goods and amongst his vast possessions was a stately mansion overlooking a beautiful valley. But there was a basic emptiness in his life. He had no religious belief, he lived alone, possessed by his possessions.

In the gate lodge at the entrance to his estate lived John, his herdsman. John was a man of simple faith and deep religious commitment. With his family he was a regular churchgoer. God's presence was a reality in his home and often at night when he opened the gate to admit his employer, the lord noticed the family on their knees in prayer.

One morning the lord was looking out on the valley resplendent in the rising sun. As he gazed on the beautiful scene, he said to himself, "It is all mine." Just then the door bell rang. Going down, he found John on the door step. "What's the matter, John?" he asked. "Are the horses all right?"

John looked embarrassed. "Yes, sir," he replied. "Sir, could I have a word with you?" He was invited on to the plush carpet, and his presence there pointed up the striking contrast between their lifestyles.

"Sir," said John hesitantly, "last night I had a dream, and in it God told me that the richest man in the valley would die tonight at midnight. I felt I should tell you. I hope, sir, that you don't mind."

"Tut . . . tut," said the lord. "I don't believe in dreams. Go on back to your work and forget it."

118

John still looked uneasy. "The dream was very vivid, sir, and the message was that the richest man in the valley would die at midnight tonight. I just had to come to you, sir, as I felt that you should know."

The lord dismissed him, but John's words bothered him so much that he finally took out his car and went to the local doctor for a check-up. The doctor examined him, pronounced him fit as a fiddle and said he'd give him another twenty years.

The lord was relieved but a lingering doubt caused him to invite the doctor around for dinner and a few drinks that evening. They enjoyed a sumptuous meal together and shortly after eleven-thirty, the doctor got up to leave. When the lord asked him to remain on for a few nightcaps, he agreed.

Eventually, when midnight passed and he was still in the land of the living, the rich man saw the doctor to the door, and then went up the stairs muttering, "Silly old John . . . upset my whole day . . . him and his damned dreams."

No sooner was he in bed than he heard the door-bell ringing. It was twelve-thirty. Going down he found a grief-stricken girl at the door whom he recognized instantly as John's teenage daughter.

"Sir," she said, looking at him through her tears, "Mummy sent me to tell you that Daddy died at midnight."

The lord froze. It was suddenly made clear to him who was the richest man in the valley.

▪ *Themes* ▪

Wealth–Wisdom–Values–Faith–Presence of God

▪ *For reflection and discussion* ▪

1. Did the ending of this story come as a surprise to you? Why, or why not?

2. In your opinion, what were the riches the herdsman had?

3. Which of the following seems best to express the wisdom in this story:
   a. Great fortunes and vast possessions are not the only kind of wealth.
   b. You can be rich without realizing it.

4. Read Luke 12:16–21. How do you make yourself rich in the sight of God?